Table of Contents

M000315118

Foreword

THIS IS THE TRUE STORY about **Ruth**, a German Mennonite girl raised in Nazi Germany. Near the end of World War II, Ruth, her mother, and Ruth's siblings became refugees in Denmark for three and a half years before being reunited with their father. During some of that time, they did not know if their father was dead or alive. In fact, for a time he was actually a prisoner of war because he had been an SS officer in Hitler's Third Reich. When the family was finally reunited, they were destitute, penniless, and needed to find a new place to call home.

It is also a story about **Mennonite Central Committee** (MCC) and the work it accomplished in war-torn Europe after World War II. Without care packages sent through MCC, the Reimer family would likely not have survived. For almost 100 years, MCC has helped displaced people find a place to call home.

This story includes one family who gave to the Reimer family—the **Daniel S. Bontrager family** of Goshen, Indiana—who invested through many letters and care packages to an unknown (to them) refugee family in Germany—and the difference their care made for this family. With six children of their own, they continued to correspond with the Reimer family and to ask for specific ways they could help meet their needs. They sent package after package for many years in the name of Christ.

The story includes **PAX** [see Appendix], a volunteer program for conscientious objectors during and after the war. Through the PAX program, lives were changed and restored. Restoration happened, not only in providing housing for refugees, but in encouraging a future hope as well.

Most importantly, this is a story about **Jehovah God**. As Ruth learned, He never leaves us nor forsakes us. As Ruth has experienced, when we belong to Him, no matter where we go, we have found a place where we belong—a place we can truly call home.

Acknowledgements

• **Linford Bontrager** for information about the Daniel Bontrager family and family photo.

• **John E. Gingerich** (September 11, 1924-February 24, 2010), former missionary to Espelkamp, Germany, for the interview he conducted (at the request of Kenneth Yoder) with Johannes and Gerda Reimer in Espelkamp, Germany (in the 1970s). From his interview, he wrote the story of Ruth and of her parents in a 60-page unpublished paper titled "The Ruth Reimer Yoder Story." Many conversations and details for this book are available because of the time he spent interviewing the Reimers and detailing the story in his account. The interview is recorded in German, and Ruth was able to listen to the conversation and verify key points. From his translation of German letters written by Johannes and Gerda Reimer to the Bontrager family (February 1947-January 1956), I was able to gain valuable information as well. These letters are numbered 1-26 and are dated from February 2, 1947-January 9, 1956.

• **Lisa Reimer Holz** and her granddaughter **Neele**—for taking photos of the autograph album and trinkets Lisa made while in Camp Hasselö. Finding dates inside this homemade autograph book helped us have a better timeline for the refugee camps in which the Reimer family lived.

• **Brad Maust** for taking the reel-to-reel tapes of Ruth's talks about her experiences and putting them on a CD (without much notice) so I could hear Ruth's story as recorded.

• **David I. Miller** (Archivist, Conservative Mennonite Conference) for providing information about dates and events pertaining to Ruth and Kenneth's talks at CMC about their post World War II experiences.

• **Rachel N. Miller** for scanning numerous photos so they could be made available for this book and emailing them to the appropriate places when requested.

• **Alice Miller Orendorf**, Archivist, who drove her vehicle through 18 inches of unplowed snow in March 2018, unlocked the door of the Casselman Valley Amish Mennonite Archives, and helped me find the reel-to-reel tapes of Ruth's first talks after she came to America in 1960.

• **Frank Peachey**, MCC U.S. Records and Library Manager, for input and information about MCC, its logo, and for access to and permission to use the MCC logo and photos as needed for this book.

• **Rachel Schrock** for taking the color photos including photos of Ruth's heirlooms that are in this book.

• **Reagan Schrock** for striking the match that ignited the flame to tell this story. He introduced the subject of a book about Ruth's story in a conversation in March 2018. This book came to be because he said, "Somebody has got to write her story!"

• **Rhoda Gingerich Sommers** for answering questions about her memories of Espelkamp and the Reimer family.

• **Cara Conner** for editing, asking questions, and giving technical advice, and helping me clarify points I had missed.

• **Ruth Emswiler** for providing edits, advice, and questions that helped make the story better.

• **Donna Beachy Kurylak** for editing with an eye for story flow and cheering Ruth's story from across the miles.

• **Kenneth and Ruth Yoder** especially for the many hours of answering questions, detailing events, sorting through photos, and educating me on German culture and language. To **Kenneth**, for caring about Ruth's story and having the foresight to hire John Gingerich to obtain information about Ruth's family through her parents in the 1970s. For sharing with me information he obtained from the Reimers in conversations with them during visits in their home in Germany and helping me understand the dichotomy of Mennonite people in Europe during both world wars. To **Ruth**, for sharing her experiences as she remembered them. For being open and vulnerable about how difficult life was and for sharing her feelings as well as facts about events (some of them personal and private) so many years later. For wanting the story to be factual without making it "better than it was or worse than it was," and helping me find the fine line to accomplish that.

A Note From the Author

This is a true story about Ruth Reimer Yoder and her family. The events are as accurate as I could make them from research, verbal interviews, video interviews, formal and informal writing, and talks that have been given in the past about or by Ruth or her parents.

Told as a biography of her time in Nazi Germany, Denmark, post-war Germany, and then America, this story is from Ruth's perspective. While the things she remembers might not coincide with others who were there, I have attempted to be true to her memories of the people and events in her life.

Conversations are frequently used to help tell the story; they are also used to interject facts as the story is told. Many conversations are based on information that came from the interviews of Ruth's parents as well as her descriptions and memories of the people in her life.

The timeline for the years in the refugee camps is an estimate. It is based on dates recorded in the interview of her parents and in the autograph book that Ruth's sister Lisa made while in Camp Hasselö, their second refugee camp in Denmark.

As a seven-year old child, I was in the audience when Ruth shared her story publicly for the first time in America. Several years later, I met her parents when they came to America to visit their daughter. I didn't grasp the importance of their story then, but now I do. Two details emblazoned themselves on my mind when I first heard Ruth's story in 1962: the buried china and the blanket used for a baby. But that's getting ahead of the story. Read on and learn for yourself about Ruth's remarkable journey.

~ Gertrude Slabach

Ruth as a cute toddler!

~ Chapter One ~
A Place in West Prussia
January 22, 1945

The winter wind howled at the windows as Ruth burrowed down under the feather covers next to her sister. It was always cold here in the winter, but this winter was colder. At least, it seemed worse than the cold winters West Prussia usually served to its people. Ruth was used to the harshness for which Grenzdorf was known. Yet the cold, this year, seemed to penetrate even deeper. Was it because of the war?

Ruth loved pleasant summer days that produced lovely flowers in this low-humidity climate near the Polish border. As she pulled the covers higher on her shoulders, she wished for summer when this flat land flourished with vegetable gardens, bushes, trees, and flowers. She wished Pappa could be home, farming the land and harvesting the many grains that were planted each year. Pappa loved his farm and the rich soil that needed no fertilizer for raising good crops. But it was winter, and Pappa was not here. He was away because of the war.

That left Mamma and the hired hands to take care of the farm without him. The farm the Reimer family lived on was one that Pappa had inherited from his father a year after his marriage. One day he would pass it on to his sons Hannie (Hans) and Dieter. Pappa and Mamma had moved into the farmhouse when they got married, and father and son farmed together. Opa and Oma Reimer [Grandpa and Grandma] continued to live in the same house with their only son and his wife. The family raised hogs, cattle, chickens, horses, and a variety of grain on the farm.

When it wasn't winter, Lisa, Hannie, and Ruth especially enjoyed playing outside. Little Dieter, not quite two, sometimes toddled after them as they played ball in the yard. Their days were filled by playing with each other and with other children. Renate and Hannelore Schultz, who lived on the neighboring farm, were frequent playmates of the Reimer children.

When it wasn't winter, the Reimers enjoyed the Laschken, a lovely, winding river. In the 1940s, there was no running water in the house, but the pump outside the house provided water for the family. Sometimes women and maids went to the Laschken to get water, carrying buckets on yokes across their shoulders. Laschken provided water for the Reimer family's cattle and their farm. The area was a delightful place in the summer when flowers and bushes bloomed around Laschken, making it as lovely as a park.

I wish this war was over! Ruth thought, pulling the covers over her head. *I wish it was summer and we could go play at the Laschken.*

But it wasn't summer. It was winter, and the Lashken was covered in ice. Holes had to be cut in the ice to get water. The ice provided a place for children and adults to skate on the river.

In addition to ice skating, bobsled riding and sleigh riding were common winter activities. Neighbors and children would join the Reimers in the winter fun. This winter it was almost too cold to be outside, and it wasn't as much fun because Pappa was gone. Just when it seemed the news and the temperatures were rising, the cold swept in again, and the Allies were getting closer.

The Laschken was not far from the farms. Oma Hintz, Ruth's maternal grandmother, lived on her farm nearby and visited often. One day, Oma Hintz planned to give her farm to her daughter's family. Pappa owned thirty hectares [74.1 acres] of land. Pappa loved the farms, and he loved his horses.

One often heard Pappa say, "A Mennonite without a farm is like a rider without a horse."[1] Pappa loved to ride his horses, and he

---

[1] Johnny Gingerich, *The Ruth Reimer, Yoder Story* (unpublished), p. 3.

The farm in West Prussia.

enjoyed spending time on the farm riding around to check on the cattle and the workers. Pappa looked quite official with his black cylinder hat, black polished boots, and his leather gloves. He belonged to Adolf Hitler's riding club even before Hitler's SS[2] was formed—before Pappa himself, a member of the Mennonite Church, joined the SS. When the Nazis had parades, Pappa would rode on one of his beautiful horses.

Servants helped with work on the farm. There were no chores for the children. Katja and Sonja were Polish workers who had been with the family for a long time. They helped with housework, gardening, and care of the children. Staschow, an older man who had a wife and children in Poland, worked for the Reimers here in Danzig. Employed on the farm for 17 years, Staschow never learned to speak German. He was a loyal worker and kept things running when Pappa was away.

Several modest houses with small plots of land were located near the farm. The people who lived there tended small gardens and

---

[2] The *Schutzstaffel* was a major paramilitary organization under Adolf Hitler and the Nazi Party (NSDAP) in Nazi Germany, and later throughout German-occupied Europe during World War II.

Lisa, Hans, and Ruth, 1942.

had a cow to provide for their families. Two or three of the tenants in these houses worked for the Reimers. Because winters in West Prussia were dry and cold, the animals had to be kept warm and bedded. When the fields were harvested and the fall plowing was finished, the hired hands concentrated on the cattle in the barn.

Ruth and Lisa with one of the cows.

Opa and Oma Reimer with Lisa in front of the house in West Prussia.

The house in which the Reimers lived was old, but stately. Its brick was kept clean, and the yard surrounding the house was immaculate. The farm was well-kept and provided for the needs of the family. As each season followed another, life had always remained the same. Until now. Until the war.

Now it was winter. Danzig's loveliness was gone, not only because it was winter, but because of the war. It had been six years since the war started, and each year was harder than the one before. This winter was proving to be particularly severe. Just west of the farm, the Vistula River and one of its branches, the Nogart River, were frozen over with a thick sheet of ice. German armies were concerned and determined to keep the Russian armies from penetrating across these frozen rivers.

This January night was no different from other long and dismal nights. It was dark, dry, and bitterly cold! The wind and coldness whirled across the landscape of what had once been a quiet and peaceful place. Each blast seemed to warn of more blizzards to come—blizzards that not only froze the landscape, but threatened to freeze hearts as well.

Always, Germany was winning the war. Always, the German soldiers were strong and mighty and kept the Russians and the Allies back. Radios had been confiscated, but village news and distributed flyers continued to shout that Germany would one day conquer the world. German soldiers confirmed the news that was heard: Germany was going to win the war!

On that dismal night in January, seven-year-old Ruth shivered under the feather tick cover as she snuggled close to Lisa, her eleven-year-old sister. *Where is Pappa?* she wondered. *When will he come home? Is he ever coming home again? Is Mamma worried? If she isn't afraid,* Ruth decided, *then I don't need to be afraid.*

It had been over a month since Ruth had seen Pappa, and even longer since he had been able to live at home. His days of coming home on weekends were over. Pappa had been home for a short visit on Christmas, and that was the last time they had seen him. Adolf Hitler had Pappa working in his army. Pappa had once been a guard in a camp in Stutthof Prison.[3] Later he stood guard at the Governor's Villa and served as an escort for important people. Ruth wasn't sure where Pappa was now or what he was doing. *Is he awake now or is he asleep in the middle of this cold night?,* she wondered. Underneath the covers and her winter clothing, Ruth began to feel sleepy, and her eyelids closed slowly as her body warmed.

The banging on the window startled the family awake. "Frau [Mrs.] Reimer, Frau Reimer! *Schnell!* [Be quick!] *Schnell!* You must hurry!" It was Herr [Mr.] Simons, one of the neighbors.

"*Was ist los?*" ["What is wrong?"] Mamma asked Herr Simons when she opened the door.

"*Achtung!* [Danger!] The Russians are coming!" Herr Simons called urgently. "They might be here by morning. You must get out tonight if you and your children will be safe! *Schnell!* [Hurry!]"

---

[3] A Nazi German concentration camp established in a secluded, wet, and wooded area near the small town of Stuthof (21 miles) east of the city of Danzig.

Oma Reimer shuffled her feet as she came into the room. "*Was ist los?*" she asked, rubbing the sleep from her eyes.

"Herr Simon said the Russians are coming, and we must go. I don't want to leave in the dark. *Ach du Lieber God!* [Oh, You dear God!] Where will we go?," Mamma asked. "Hans told me not to travel on the road because we will only die. It is so cold, and where would we go? Where would we stay?" Mamma wrung her hands, her face full of dismay and worry.

Oma nodded. "It is not safe for you to go now. Tomorrow we will see what we can do. Maybe the Russians will be held back. Surely Hitler's men will keep them back!" Oma's voice did not sound hopeful.

"Shhh, children," Mamma said when she came into the room to check on her girls and saw Ruth and Lisa sitting up in their beds. "Be still so you don't wake Dieter. Go back to sleep. It will be all right."

"What are we going to do?" Lisa asked, wide awake.

"We're going to go back to sleep. Tomorrow we will decide what we should do. Just go to sleep and don't worry, girls," Mamma said, rubbing her hand slowly across her abdomen. She waited a few minutes until she was sure her girls would not disturb anybody, then she tiptoed out of the room.

Is Mamma sick? Ruth wondered. *She keeps rubbing her stomach. What will we do if Mamma gets sick?* Oma Reimer was too old to take care of them; plus, she had to take care of Opa, who was paralyzed from a stroke. Oma Hintz would not be able to take care of them, either. Now Pappa wasn't here. *What will we do if the Russians come?*

Nobody wanted the Russians to come. They were mean to women and to children and burned their houses and barns. Ruth remembered the day an air strike had hit the neighbor's barn. Airplanes dropped sulfur over the buildings, and before they knew it, everything was in flames. Equipment normally available was now needed for the war, so there was nothing that could be done. There was no help to be had, and the barn had continued to burn. The Reimer children, standing behind their barn on the frozen manure pile, had watched the flames shoot high into the sky. The wood gurgled and crackled, splintering as it toppled into ash heaps on the ground. Ruth stood shivering even as the intense heat reached across the field to finger her skin.

The Russians bombed places and didn't care who was living there. At first, their air raids were sporadic and infrequent, and it was safe to play outside. Later, when the air raids started again, they became more frequent. Mamma instructed her children to run to the house or the barn whenever they heard the sirens announcing an air raid.

No matter what they were doing or where they were playing, Ruth and her siblings dropped everything and ran inside as soon as they heard the shrill sound of sirens. Sometimes they ran to the barn if it was closer. Other times they dashed to the house, huddling together in the basement with Mamma and the others until the sirens stopped.

"We must have all the lights turned off at nighttime," Mamma explained. "That way, the airplanes won't see where we live when they fly over us to drop bombs. If we keep the lights off, we will be safer."

Night after night, Mamma and the children listened to the airplanes flying over their land. Night after night, they listened to gunfire and heard bombs being dropped on neighboring buildings. There was rifle and mortar fire. The Russians were getting closer. What was going to happen to them? Only God knew.

The war had impacted even the schoolroom and the teachers. Ruth's first year of school had begun nine months ago on the first of April. Just when Ruth was learning to read, schools were closed because of the war. Most of the teachers were men who had now joined the army, and without teachers, schools could not reopen after the Christmas break. In addition, it wasn't safe to travel from home

Pappa had refused to join the National Socialistic Party, which made it more difficult to buy farm equipment. Because farmers were extremely important to Hitler and because he needed them to take care of his army, he cancelled all farming debts and reformed trade relations to benefit the German farmers. This made the farmers part of the privileged class.[7] Even though Pappa was a farmer, he did not benefit from Hitler's action because he refused to join their party. He could, however, be a part of the Riding SS without being a Party member and still be respected when he needed to make farm purchases.[8]

Initially, Pappa had been able to come home to visit. At first, he was recruited by the village police to help guard the bridges which were an easy target for sabotage. This assignment was in August of 1939 before the war broke out on the first of September. The longer the war lasted, the less time Pappa could get away to come home. Now he was kept busy, but his family did not always know where he was. Sometimes he stood guard at the Governor's Villa near the Baltic Sea in Danzig as a sentry. This villa was guarded day and night by three SS men in eight-hour shifts.[9]

"I just have to walk around the grounds during the day, and sometimes at night," Pappa had told his family the previous summer of 1944. "Sometimes I guard high-ranking officials who come to the Villa."

Once there was a parade in Poland honoring the *Fürher* [Leader]. Pappa rode in the second car behind Adolf Hitler in that parade.[10] Pappa believed that Hitler was going to make Germany—and all the world—a better place. Along with other Mennonite men, he felt that he had no choice but to join the Nazi party. The other option would have been to refuse, be lined up along a wall, and be shot.[11]

---

[7] Dean Taylor, "Mennonite Nazis: A Lesson from History." Accessed May 27, 2018. [http://www.ephrataministries.org/remnant-2012-11-mennonite-nazis.a5w]
[8] Gingerich, p. 15.
[9] Gingerich, p. 17.
[10] Kenneth Yoder conversation with author, Fall 2018.
[11] *Ibid.*

Pappa in his uniform with Mamma, Lisa, Ruth, and Hans. Dieter is not pictured—possibly sleeping.

Even though Pappa was a Mennonite and went to church, he didn't spend a lot of time reading the Bible. In the Reimer home, the Bible stayed on a shelf until Christmas time, when it was brought down so Pappa could read the Christmas story to his family. Along with other Germans, Pappa had bought Adolf Hitler's book *Mein Kampf,* [*My Struggle*] which was a required purchase for all German citizens. Every couple who got married was given a copy of this book. Next to the Bible, this book had the highest sales in all of Germany. The Reimer family did not pray at mealtimes, but the children were taught to pray before they went to bed.

Sometimes Pappa found another way to come home to visit. That previous summer, he brought people to help work in the fields on his farm. He stood guard over the people while they worked in the fields.

"Who are these people?" Ruth asked Mamma. "Why are they prisoners?"

"Shhh, little girl," Mamma whispered, looking at the floor. "Don't ask any questions."

Day after day, men and women were brought out to work in Pappa's fields. In the evening, they were taken away. Their faces looked sad, and they didn't smile or talk much. Sometimes she watched the men look around the farm, eyeing the guards and the edge of the fields. She wondered what they were thinking, but she didn't ask questions anymore. All she knew was that they were prisoners—Germans who were prisoners. What have they done wrong? If Mamma didn't want to talk about it, then surely Pappa wouldn't answer her questions. Sometimes Pappa was there in his uniform, watching the people, but she couldn't ask him. Sometimes other soldiers came to guard the prisoners as they worked in their fields. Ruth quit asking questions, but she always wondered about these people and what they had done wrong to cause them to be prisoners.

Maybe, Ruth pondered, *they are Jewish.* Once Ruth had asked Mamma why the German people did not like the Jews.

"Why did they break the windows in their stores?" she asked.

Ruth had heard about *Kristallnacht* [Crystal Night] because the Germans still talked and laughed about that night. They still thought that the Jews were not good people.

"People think the Jews are rich and greedy," Mamma said. "Martin Luther[12] said they are greedy,[13] and we have to deal with them," Mamma explained.

"What is *Kristallnacht*?" Ruth asked Mamma.

---

[12] A church reformer of the 16th century.

[13] Harry Westerink. "Church Reformer Luther Inspired Hitler." In De Bewoonde Vrouw. Accessed Sept. 23, 2018. http://www.doorbraak.eu/geblader-te/30142v01.htm

Mamma sighed, and didn't say anything for a bit. Then she answered, "The year you were born, the Germans had *Kristallnacht*. All throughout Germany, people broke the windows of Jewish shopkeepers at night. Because people thought the Jews were greedy, they threw rocks through the glass windows of their stores. This was to punish them for being greedy and to make them shut down their businesses so they wouldn't have money and wouldn't be rich. There didn't seem to be anything they could do because they were, after all, Jewish."

"What did the police do?" Ruth asked.

Mamma was quiet for a moment. Then she replied, "The police did not do anything."

Ruth sat quietly, thinking about what Mamma had said. It didn't make sense to her; but if Pappa thought this was right, then surely it was.

Pappa wore his uniform when he came home to visit. He had to because it was an order. Soldiers were to always wear their uniforms, but they were not allowed to wear them to church. Therefore, soldiers were to remove their names from church membership since they could not go to church in their uniforms and were never to remove their uniforms. Pappa couldn't go to church because this was Hitler's order, but he never removed his name from church membership.

"Some of the East and West Prussian pastors feel it is the duty of the Mennonite Church to also help with the war effort to bring stability to Europe," Pappa had explained.

When Opa Hintz died in June 1942, Pappa came home for the funeral. He did so under potential penalty from the government. "I asked for an exceptional pass to come," Pappa told Mamma. "They would not grant me the request, so I came home with a regular pass."

"What are you going to do?" Mamma asked Pappa. "You can't go to the church in your uniform, and you will be in trouble if you take it off."

"I am going to your father's funeral in my suit," Pappa's voice was strong. "When I come back, I will put my uniform on again."

When they went to Opa Hintz's funeral, Pappa had to walk past the SS command post where other soldiers saw him. He looked straight ahead and did not speak to the soldiers. The soldiers did not talk to him when they saw him walking past.

When Pappa returned home, he put his soldier's uniform on and went back to work. None of the soldiers reported him, but some of them laughed at him. Ruth and her siblings were too young to understand the risk Pappa took that day, but Mamma did.

"Now, what did the priest say, Johannes?"[14] one of them asked, slapping his knee with his hand. Others joined the volley of laughter. Pappa knew that the less he said, the better. What he had done was a dangerous breach of authority, and he waited anxiously to see if he would be reported. To his relief, even though the soldiers made fun of him, they did not report him to the authorities.

Pappa did not obey the order to remove himself from church membership. He kept meticulous records of his activities as a soldier in his *Soldbuch* [identification book].[15] He even wrote down that he attended church for the funeral of his father-in-law. Even though he was ordered by his superiors to remove himself from church membership, he did not comply.

Pappa's own father had refused to serve in World War I. Herman Reimer was a conscientious objector and served as a non-combatant recruit. As a member of the Mennonite Church in Prussia, he held to the same beliefs as his church. But this was World War II. Some Mennonite leaders felt that Hitler was going to do such good that they needed to support the *Führer* [leader]. Ruth heard the conversations among her elders and knew Hitler was an important man. Even though she couldn't understand everything, she knew that the Mennonites of Germany were happy with their new *Führer*. So happy, in fact, that they had sent a telegram[16] to him. Written September

---

[14] Gingerich, p. 16.
[15] The *Soldbuch* is a soldier's personal identification in wartime.
[16] Dean Taylor.

10, 1933, the telegram said:

> ### To Chancellor Adolf Hitler, Berlin:
>
> *The Conference of East and West Prussian Mennonites, assembled today in Tiegenhagen, Free State of Danzig, feels deep gratitude for the powerful revival that God has given our nation through your energy, and promises joyful cooperation in the upbuilding of our Fatherland through the power of the Gospel, faithful to the motto of our forefathers: No other foundation can anyone lay than that which is laid which is Jesus Christ.*

While it is unlikely that Adolf Hitler replied to all telegrams he received, he did respond to this one.

> *For your loyalty and your readiness to cooperate in the upbuilding of the German nation, expressed in your letter to me, I express my sincere thanks.   - Adolf Hitler*

Now it was 1945, fifteen years later. So much had happened that people didn't expect. Now, Pappa was in the war, helping Hitler. Mamma was at home with the children, waiting for a baby to come, a baby that Pappa didn't even know about. Mamma and her children were hoping that Pappa would be able to come home before long. Things were so different now, and it was all because of the war.

Lisa, Ruth, and Hans, about 1940.

~ *Chapter Two* ~

A PLACE FOR STRANGERS

February - April 1945

The loud, insistent knock at the door commanded a response. Mamma opened the door to find a German colonel waiting impatiently.

"*Guten tag*, [Good day] Frau Reimer," he spoke brusquely. "We will use your place for my headquarters. I need to see your rooms."

Hurriedly, Mamma opened the door of her *Grosse Stube* [large living room]. This room was used only for special occasions, which included Christmas, birthdays, or entertaining special guests.

"You are welcome to stay in here," she showed the officer inside.

The colonel strode into the room, standing straight and tall with his hands on his belt. He surveyed the furnishings of the *Grosse Stube*.

"I will take this room for my office, and we will be using your kitchen as well." He marched across the room and peered out the window. "My soldiers will sleep here when necessary or in the barn. My soldiers will need food to eat, and they will eat before the rest of you do."

Mamma nodded again. There was no reason to argue. These were German soldiers, and they might even know Pappa.

Soon more soldiers came. They slept on the cement floor in the *waschküche* [laundry room]. Sometimes the soldiers fixed their own food, and sometimes they ate what Oma Reimer fixed for the family. The soldiers ate what they wanted and left the rest for the family. There was enough food, but not too much. The children knew better than to complain. The soldiers might not be happy if they complained.

At night, the German soldiers slept in the house—their headquarters. In the morning, they left to do their job in protecting their country and fighting the enemy. There were as many as ten or fifteen soldiers, but the children were not afraid. The soldiers' uniforms were the same as other German uniforms. These men worked for Hitler, and they were not the enemy.

It was the Russians whom they feared. If the Russians came, they would be mean to women and girls. They would take livestock and money. The Russians would take their homes and their possessions. It was the Russians who took children from their parents and put them in orphanages. It was the Russians who burned down buildings and barns. These Nazi soldiers were not like those Russians! They were kind to Mamma and her children.

"Come see the cannon," one of the soldiers told the Reimer children one afternoon.

The children hurried to Pappa's field, where the soldiers had set up a cannon.

"Look through here," one of them said.

Hannie bent down and looked inside the cannon.

"We will use this to protect our country," the soldier said. "We will not let those Russians take over our country," he spit on the ground.

"*Ja Wohl,* [yes, certainly,] another one said. "With this cannon, we can shoot down to the Vistula River if any of the Russians try to come across there!"

April came. The fighting was getting nearer. Neighbors talked about the war. There was a lot happening that was talked about in hushed tones among themselves. Yet, the soldiers always declared that Germany was winning the war.

Ruth remembered the expression of the soldier the day he showed them the cannon. He was determined, so Ruth was certain

Germany would win the war. Even though spring was warming up the countryside, death and destruction were nearer and more frightening. Home wasn't home anymore, thanks to the war.

One day Mamma gave Ruth permission to play with Alice, and since it was too cold to be outside, Ruth played with her in the living room. Sometimes playing with Alice helped her forget the war. She loved holding and rocking the doll and singing to her. The house was quiet on this April morning, and for a few moments, Ruth forgot about the war.

Suddenly, a blast of cold air entered the house as the door opened. Two of the soldiers came into the house and stomped into the kitchen. Mamma never locked the doors anymore, because the soldiers needed to be able to come and go as they pleased. The soldiers helped themselves to coffee. Mamma hurried to make more coffee for the soldiers.

"*Wir waren letzte Nacht in einem Wasserkocher* [We were in a kettle last night,]" one of them said, taking a long gulp of coffee. "The Allies were coming in from the west, and the Russian army was coming in from the east. They nearly made a break through and would have crossed the river last night, but we held them back!" He chuckled. "There are many Russian bodies floating on the Weichsel River. They tried to get to the Baltic Sea, but we held them back from the shore, or they would have established a beachhead and been able to make an invasion."

He filled his cup again. "Yes, we held them back! I cannot imagine how many men we would have lost if they had advanced! If I were you, Frau Reimer, I would leave with my family."

The other soldier shook his head, "I don't know that I would advise that because the roads are full of ruts. It is cold, and you won't be able to get through because there are so many people trying to leave. Today I saw men and women and even small children pulling hand wagons. One mother was crying because her baby froze to death while she was walking." He shook his head sadly. "It just got too cold."

"Yes," the first soldier said, "Refugees moving out are picking up half-frozen children who are roaming the streets. I told them to take them to any houses that are still occupied."

He poured more coffee into his cup and continued, "We are enlisting more men. More soldiers are coming in, and the roads are full of people. We have a new weapon in these hand grenades. We are giving the grenades to the *Volksturm Soldaten* [storm troops]. We are telling them, 'With these grenades, we will win the war!'"

"Yet people are leaving Prussia," the second soldier admitted. "They are saying that soon it will not be safe for women and children to be here. Older people will probably not be hurt," he glanced at Oma Hintz who had come into the kitchen. "But people are leaving, heading out of the country just in case the Russians break through."

"I have seen flyers telling women and children to leave," Mamma mentioned.

"Flyers?" one of the soldiers raised his eyebrows.

"Yes, our airplanes are dropping flyers from the sky. The flyers say that all women and children should prepare to leave." Mamma's voice trembled, just a little. "Where are the people going who are leaving?" Mamma asked. "Where is the safest place to go?"

"You will need to head toward the interior of Germany, because the Russians are being held back there. Or, you can go to the Baltic Sea," he answered. "But don't try to cross the Weichsel River on foot. The ice is not deep enough, and people have fallen through and drowned."

"The military has the right of way, so all refugees must make way for our soldiers. It's snowing now and the road will be even harder to travel. There are so many pieces of broken wagons. There are dead horses and cattle along the road. It would be slow going, and you might just get stuck with all the others. You should just stay here for now," the other soldier suggested, tapping his foot on the cold kitchen floor.

Mamma listened carefully to the soldiers. Without Pappa to talk to, she welcomed advice from the soldiers who seemed to know what was best. For now, she would stay here.

Sometimes German soldiers captured allied men. Often, they were taken to prison, but one day a soldier brought two prisoners to the house. "These are French prisoners of war," the soldier told Mamma. "They will live here and help you with your farm."

Now Mamma had more people to feed; but she also had more workers to help take care of the farm and the animals. One of the prisoners could speak some German. The other one didn't speak German, but he seemed to understand what was said. One never knew if he really couldn't understand the language or just chose not to speak the German language!

When this prisoner was spoken to, his only response was always, "*Ja Wohl.*" [Yes, certainly]. Before long, the children referred to him simply as *Ja Wohl.*

Mamma's farmhouse seemed to be full all the time. The French prisoners were happy to be there instead of in a prison camp. They worked willingly and never attempted an escape. Mamma was kind to the prisoners and was not afraid of them, and neither were her children.

Many refugees were traveling through the Danzig area. Trying to get as far away as they could, they headed for the border. As the horses grew more tired and frail due to lack of food, the refugees tossed out furniture and other items too heavy for the horses. Roadways were rutted from the buggy tracks and strewn with housekeeping items, blankets, clothes, and feed for the horses that had not been able to survive. Sometimes horses were unhitched, and their owners continued alone on foot.

Mamma's face was sober, even more than it used to be. The lines around her face from where she smiled had disappeared. She always seemed preoccupied. Sometimes she stood in the doorway of the house, looking across the field, her hand resting on her abdomen. *What is she thinking about?* Ruth wondered. *Does she miss Pappa? Is she sick? Will the baby be okay?*

Oma Reimer with Hans, Lisa, and Ruth.

Mamma did not complain. If she was worried, she never said so. Each day remained the same. The workers and prisoners took care of the farm. Mamma took care of the house with the assistance of Oma Reimer who also helped with washing and cooking.

Opa and Oma Reimer had always lived in this house, and now Oma did a lot of the cooking. Opa couldn't help because he was an invalid and spent his time in their bedroom. He couldn't walk, talk, or feed himself, so Oma made sure he was well cared for. When Oma wasn't cooking for the family and the soldiers, she spent her time in the room with him. They ate together in their bedroom at the back of the house.

Oma Hintz came to see her daughter as often as she could. She wanted to see for herself how Mamma was doing, especially since there would be a new baby in several months. One day when she visited, she had some news for Mamma.

"Gerda, your *Tante* [Aunt] Grete is coming to move in with me," Oma told Mamma.

"Tante Grete?," Mamma asked, surprised.

"Yes, Gerda," Oma Hintz said. "She feels it is becoming more unsafe in the city, so I told her to come and live with me. She is coming tomorrow."

"It will be nice for you to have someone staying with you, especially with the war going on," Mamma said.

Oma nodded. "And she is bringing a boy with her when she comes."

"A boy?" Mamma wondered.

"Yes, his parents both died from the war. He is all alone. His name is Heinz, and he has been living with Grete. He has no one."

"How old is he?," Mamma asked.

"Grete said she is not sure, but he appears to be 12 or 13."

"Of course," Mamma responded. "I am glad she can be of help to the poor boy."

"Yes," Oma replied, "it seems that things are going to get worse before they get better. I will be glad to have my sister here. We can keep each other company. I am sure the boy will be of help, and I do feel sorry for him, being an orphan."

Ruth with both Omas: Oma Reimer on the left and Oma Hintz on the right.

It seemed that everywhere people from the city were moving to the country to live with relatives because it was safer there. Oma Reimer's sister Eliese and her husband Herman Bergen had come to live with her. The fighting in their city had grown so much worse that they feared for their safety. So, they moved into the country with the Reimers. *Onkel* [Uncle] Herman was not in good health, and Tante Eliese knew taking care of him would be even more difficult in the city. Now both Omas had sisters who had moved to the country from the city because of the war.

Now Mamma had not only the French prisoners of war and the German soldiers in her house. She also had Onkel Herman and Tante Eliese sharing accommodations.

Even so, it seemed the visitors kept coming. Mamma never knew who next would show up at her door. One day there was another knock at the door. Another traveler?

"Good afternoon," Mamma said to the stranger at the door.

"Good afternoon," the stranger replied. "I am Frau Noetzel, and these are my children."

"What can I do for you?" Mamma asked Frau Noetzel, smiling at the children.

"My children and I are alone. Renate is two and Marianne is five," Frau Noetzel said, patting each child on the head. We need a place to stay," she begged. "Is there any chance we can stay with you?" Mamma opened the door further.

"Come in," she said. "We will share with you what we have; it isn't much, but there is shelter here."

"Oh, Danke, Danke [thank you, thank you]," Frau Noetzel said. "How can I ever thank you?"

More children to play with and to eat their food! More people who needed a place to stay. For the next months, the children played together. If they were outside and heard the sirens, they ran to the house or to the barn—whichever was closest.

The fighting was getting closer, and the soldiers who came to their house sometimes slammed the front door when they came in. They clomped across the floor and grabbed coffee oftener than they had when they first moved into the Reimer's house.

Maybe they are tired, Ruth thought. *Or maybe they are worried. They surely seem grumpy! If the Germans are still winning the war, then why do they seem so worried?* Ruth was puzzled.

Any time, day or night, the door of the house might open. They listened for footsteps. It was easy to tell when the steps belonged to a man—a soldier. Was it a German soldier or an enemy soldier? The family breathed a sigh of relief when they heard the soldier speak in German. He was one of theirs, and there was no need to be afraid.

There were plenty of bedrooms because now Mamma and the children shared a room. Even with the soldiers in the house, there was room for the Opas, Frau Noetzl, and her children, Onkel Herman and Tante Eliese and the two French prisoners. Hannie was just younger than Lisa and older than Ruth. Little Dieter was nearly age two. Now all of them—Mamma and her children—slept in the same room at night.

"Because," Mamma said, "we will all stay together now so that we are ready. We will wear our clothes and coats to go to bed, and keep our shoes here on the floor," she had explained. "Then if we have to leave in a hurry, we will be ready."

Mamma was calm when she talked about what must be done, just in case. She didn't seem afraid, so Ruth wasn't afraid. Yet, sometimes she wondered when this war would end. *When will Pappa come home? Will he ever come home again?*

Now they stayed inside the house and kept a suitcase packed in case they had to leave in the night. They slept in their coats in the same room. It was not just because they needed to be ready to leave at any minute, Ruth learned. It was also so they could die together. What if an airplane dropped a bomb on their farm?

"If we are all together, then if one of us dies, we will all die together," Mamma explained. Sometimes Ruth lay awake at night, wondering what it would be like if a bomb was dropped on their house. *What will it be like for Pappa if all us die together? Then he will have no one,* Ruth thought.

~ *Chapter Three* ~

A PLACE OF BURIALS

February - April 1945

While it seemed that death could happen to them at any time, each morning they awoke, glad to have made it through the night without another air raid. There was still food to eat and the weather was getting warmer. Maybe it was a sign that times would get better!

Onkel Herman was not well, and that was another reason Tante Eliese wanted to be with her family. She did not want to be left alone if he died. Each day he seemed to get weaker, and it was not surprising to any of the adults when Onkel Herman died. Tante Eliese seemed almost relieved. Now she wouldn't have to worry about what to do with her sick husband if the Russians invaded their country.

"Well now, Onkel Herman won't have to suffer through the war," Hannie told Ruth.

"We will have the funeral at the church," Mamma said. Ruth remembered the last time there was a funeral. It was for Opa Hintz. When Opa Hintz died on June 26, 1942, Pappa was able to come home. That was almost three years ago; but this time, Pappa wouldn't be coming home. He was busy with the war.

This time, the enemy planes were flying overhead. This time, it was not safe to be out on the road. The wagon was ready with the casket when another siren blasted through the March air. It was another air raid, right near their farm.

So, Mamma changed their plans. She said, "We will bury Onkel Herman in the garden."

Quickly, she called for the hired men to dig a grave in the garden.

Against the backdrop of planes flying overhead, against the possibility of bombs being dropped, the short service was held at the house, and Onkel Herman was buried in the garden. Tante Eliese was now a widow.

A few days later, a wagon pulled into the yard. The man trudged slowly to the door of the house. His forehead showed lines of tiredness and worry.

"We need a place to stay, Frau, bitte, [please]" he begged. "My daughter is sick, and my wife is tired."

By this time, Mamma was used to having people stop in unannounced. Sometimes they needed to give their horses rest for the night. Sometimes the travelers were too tired to keep going. Sometimes the travelers went on without their horses and just left them to roam the countryside. Food was important, and it was more important that the travelers have food than their horses, so the horses were left to fend for themselves. Many people could not make the journey and died. As the dead were being buried, their clothing was passed on to others who needed it in the cold of this fading winter.

This, Ruth thought, is what war does to us all.

Always, Mamma let the travelers stay for the night. The horses were put in the barn and the travelers stayed in the house. This time was no different.

"Come in, come in," Mamma invited, opening the door.

Ruth looked at the little girl. Was she five years old? Maybe four? Maybe six? She looked so cold, sad, and sick. She never stopped whimpering as her father carried her into the house.

"Why won't she be quiet?," Hannie asked Mamma that night. "She just cries and cries."

"Hush, son," Mamma replied. "She is sick. They need to be able to rest. Maybe by morning she will feel better. At least they have a warm place to stay tonight," she said, pulling the blankets over him.

All during the night, the children were awakened by the cries of the child. *Will she ever stop crying?! I'm glad we can give them a warm place,* Ruth thought. *Maybe by morning the little girl will feel better. Maybe then she will stop crying.*

In the darkness, Ruth could hear the voice of the little girl's mamma, trying to soothe her child. Sometimes the cries were a whimper, and other times she wailed. I wish she could go to sleep, Ruth thought. *I'm sure if she goes to sleep, she will feel better in the morning.* Finally, Ruth put her head under her pillow to muffle the sound and was able to go back to sleep.

Darkness gave way to light as cold seeped through the house. It was early morning, and this time the quiet awakened Ruth. She sat up in bed with a start. Why was everything so still?! It was too quiet! Something must be wrong.

The little girl was no longer crying, but someone else was. Ruth heard sobbing coming from the next room. Then the voice of the father came through the stillness, talking in low tones to his wife. His voice quavered, and now Ruth could hear him crying. Why were they both crying, she wondered? As their crying became muffled, Ruth wondered what was wrong.

Mamma tiptoed into the room. Her face was sad as she shook her head at her children.

"Shhh," she motioned with her finger to her mouth. "You must be quiet. Let the mother and the father alone. Their little girl died during the night."

"What?" Lisa whispered, sitting up in bed. "Why did she die?"

"I don't know," Mamma answered soberly. "I think she had been too cold for too long. Her father thinks she froze to death. We will stay in here for a little bit so they can be alone," she sighed.

Ruth and Lisa looked at each other as Hannie sat up in bed, rubbing his eyes. They shivered as they crawled out from under the covers. The floor felt cold as they slipped into their shoes. On that bleak morning, the house was somber. Outside, the sky was gray and barren. Cloudy skies dared anyone to smile or to feel warmth—or to be unafraid. Mamma and the children said goodbye to the parents and watched as they walked out of the house, the father carrying the body of his little girl in his arms. Mamma's face showed such sadness and grief. As she went about her work that day, Mamma looked weary and forlorn. Ruth wished again that Pappa were here. If Pappa were here, Mamma would not be so sad or so tired. Pappa would help Mamma smile, if only he were here.

Another day, new German soldiers showed up at the house. The soldiers saluted briskly as Mamma opened the door. Without any introductions, they asked Mamma if there were any invalids in the house. Mamma nodded her head slowly.

She opened the door and allowed the soldiers inside. It didn't take them long to find Opa in his bed. Opa opened his eyes and looked at the soldiers. He could understand what they were saying even though he couldn't talk to them.

"We will take him where he can get better. All sick people must go away. If the Russians come, they will kill him. This way he will be safe," one of the soldiers explained.

"*Ja Wohl,*" [Yes, certainly,] another soldier said. "This is no place for someone like him. We will get him out of here so he will be safe."

The soldiers set about fixing blankets to carry Opa outside. It was obvious by the way the soldiers were acting that this was not a decision the family could make. It had already been decided, and the soldiers simply came to do their job.

"They are going to take you where you will be safe, Hermann," Oma told Opa, clutching his hand. Ruth saw that Oma's hands were trembling as she hugged her husband one last time. The soldiers waited while the children and Mamma told Opa good-bye. Opa couldn't talk, but he allowed them to touch his hands and tell him goodbye. *When will we see Opa again? Where will we find him after the war? Is he ever coming back?* Ruth wondered.

Mamma didn't talk much about the war, and she didn't say what she was thinking. She kept her children inside as much as possible. If she allowed them to go outside, they had to stay close to the house so they could hear her if she called.

Ruth overheard one of the soldiers talking to Mamma. "There are children out there roaming the streets. Some of them got lost from their parents, and some of them probably don't have parents anymore. Make sure you keep your children inside," he warned her.

After hearing what the soldiers said to Mamma, Ruth wasn't surprised when Mamma gathered her children together. "You children need to stay inside," Mamma told them. "There are so many people out there, and some of them are sick. We need to stay inside where we are safer. We never know when a bomb from the enemy might come."

"The Americans and British are moving in closer from the west," a soldier informed her another day. "I don't know how much longer you should stay. When you decide to leave, don't travel by land. It might take you right into the allied front where there is active fighting. Go by way of the sea. You can go to Denmark. They say they are neutral, but it is occupied by our forces now," he suggested.

A few weeks later, the German soldiers packed their gear and left. The general cleaned his belongings out of the *Grosse Stube* and told Mamma and the children goodbye. He seemed to be in a hurry to leave as he saddled his horse and rode away.

That spring, Mamma buried the Rosentaler China in the yard by the lilac bush with the help of her hired hands. The trunk with the rifles and fur coats was safely hidden under the floor of the barn.

When Mamma came back, she would dig up her things, at least if no one had taken them. Now that the hired help and Staschow knew where her things were buried, would they be content to leave them there for her return, or would they help themselves in her absence? If the Omas stayed on the farm, the items would be safe in the ground. But what if the Omas had to leave? What if they got sick, or died before Mamma and the children came back? Would someone else find the things she had buried, or would they be safe? Mamma could only hope it would be so.

~ Chapter Four ~

A PLACE ON THE BALTIC SEA

April 28 - May 10, 1945

"Children," Mamma said on the morning of April 28, "it is time for us to go. We need to pack our things."

"Where are we going?" asked Ruth.

"We are going to head to the Baltic Sea, and then go to Denmark."

"How will we get there?" Hannie asked. "Pappa said not to take the horse and wagon."

"We will find a way," Mamma said as she filled a container with oil for cooking.

Oma Hintz had come to the house that morning to tell her daughter goodbye. Tante Grete came, too, and brought Heinz with her. They busied themselves, helping Mamma get things packed and put away.

"Are Oma Reimer and Oma Hintz coming with us?" Lisa asked, looking at the calendar. "It has been three months since Herr Simons thought we should leave. At least it is warmer now."

Oma Hintz and Oma Reimer shook their heads. "We are too old," Oma Hintz said. "They won't hurt old women like us. We will stay here and take care of the farm for you."

Mamma nodded. "But Heinz is going to go with us. Tante Greta will stay with Oma Hintz and Tante Eliese will stay with Oma Reimer. Each of you will have a small satchel with a change of clothing. I know it is spring, but you will wear two coats. It might be colder where we are going." She looked at Hans. "Help me get the alcohol burner ready, Hannie," Mamma instructed.

Lisa and Hannie helped Mamma get the food items ready: lard for bread, an alcohol burner and more alcohol for cooking, rice, and bread. Hannie put the suitcase and food items into Dieter's baby carriage. Mamma tucked a blanket into the baby carriage.

"I want to take our dishes," Lisa told Ruth. "Go get them so I can pack them."

Ruth scurried to get the sets of dishes that belonged to her and her sister. The dishes Lisa wanted were sets of two plates and cups that had been given to each of them for Christmas. Carefully, Lisa placed the dishes between newspapers and added them to the things Mamma was taking.

Staschow was helpful in getting everything loaded.

"Come with us so you can be safe," Mamma said.

"No, I will stay here," Staschow replied. "I am old, and I am a

One of the plates packed by Lisa and Ruth.

Pole. The soldiers won't bother me. Don't worry about your farm, Frau Reimer," Staschow said. "I will be here, and I will look after things."

Staschow was faithful and loyal. Mamma knew that she could trust him. Katja and Sonja scurried around the kitchen, getting things together for Mamma to pack. That morning, Staschow loaded the wagon with the baby carriage, food, and satchels. Mamma had sewed three tiny knapsacks for her older children. Mamma put each child's savings account book as well as a little bit of money inside each knapsack. She also included a paper with each child's name and age. She hung the 6"x4" knapsacks around their necks.

"This is so if you get lost, others will know who you are and how to find me," she explained, placing the string of the knapsack around Ruth's neck and tucking the knapsack inside her shirt. "Sometimes children get separated from their parents, and nobody knows who they are. This way, anyone who wants to help you will know who you are."

Oma Reimer and Oma Hintz hugged Mamma and the children. Somberly, the family stepped up into the wagon. Lisa carried Dieter onto the wagon and put him in the buggy. Mamma put her arms around Hannie and Ruth. Heinz waved to Tante Eliese as he climbed into the wagon. Frau Noetzel and her children found seats in the wagon with the others.

Staschow climbed up on the seat of the wagon. He would take them to the Baltic Sea, and then he would return. No one seemed worried that he would try to escape.

"Giddyap!" Staschow snapped the reins over the horses' backs.

"Bye, Oma!" the children waved.

The Omas and Tante Eloise waved goodbye. Frau Noetzel waved goodbye. Mamma and the children waved goodbye, and Heinz waved goodbye to Tante Eloise as she stood in the yard. *Why is Oma Reimer crying?* Ruth wondered. *Is she afraid? When will we see her again?*

The road to the Baltic Sea was littered with household goods left behind by Germans hurrying to leave the country. Roaming cattle searched for food while bloated animal carcasses sprawled along the roads. Weary travelers trudged on the roadway, almost too tired and frail to make the journey, sometimes needing to step over or around dead bodies. Ruts in the road made it difficult to maneuver, but the horses kept going.

Charred buildings still smoldered, burning Ruth's nostrils and adding to the stench as they drove away from Danzig. The air was putrid with smoke and the bleakness of death. Dieter wrinkled his nose. "Stinky, stinky!" he said, covering it with his small hands.

Ruth knew the sea was closer when she smelled its icy waters. Other travelers blocked their view, yet the smell of cold death lingered in the frigid, dismal air. They had seen such despair and gloom on this short trip on the wagon. Things had changed so much. Everything was dismal. The loveliness was gone. *This*, Ruth thought, *is all because of the war.*

The wagon was full with the seven children and two women: Mamma, Lisa, Hannie, Ruth, and Dieter; Heinz; and Frau Noetzel and her children. People hurried along, all heading to the Baltic Sea. It was the only way to get out of Germany as the Americans and Russians were getting closer. The Russians, especially, made Mamma want to get out of her beloved Germany. Soon they would be at the Baltic Sea.

Maybe also soon we will be able to see Pappa again. Or, will we ever see him again? Ruth wondered. In the distance was the Baltic Sea. Finally! It was exciting to see, for soon they would make passage and find a place to be safe if the Russians invaded their country.

At the port, Mamma was told, "You need a Ferry to take you over to Hela Harbor, and then there you can board the big ship to take you to the west. There is no Ferry going tonight anymore, although a freighter will take you there."

Mamma was dismayed! Her face showed her consternation. Yet, there was nothing she could do, so, along with other people trying to flee their country, Mamma and the children waited with Frau Noetzel and her children and Heinz. It seemed to take a long time until the freighter came.

The first thing Mamma noticed when the freighter docked by the shore was that there were no railings! They were going to get on a boat with their children, and there were no railings! There was no other choice, so Mamma and her children, Frau Noetzel and her children, and Heinz got on board the freighter. Mamma looked around, trying to decide what to do. She tied one end of her blanket to the baby carriage and put the blanket around the backs of her children. She held onto the other end of the blanket, providing a guardrail of sorts. If any of them started to fall, the blanket would catch them.

The guards warned them about others who had fallen into the water. "One man fell into the water with a heavy coat on, and it pulled him down," a guard told them as they boarded the boat.

"Watch your children," he said to the mothers. Lisa put Dieter into the buggy and then sat down next to her siblings, keeping her hand on Dieter to make sure he would not try to climb out. The guard looked at Hannie. "Be sure to sit very still," he said as he patted Hannie on the head.

Slowly, the freighter pulled out of the harbor and set sail for Hela Harbor. Overhead, the night sky lit the way across the water. Ruth felt her eyes drooping. It had been a long day. So much had happened since this morning when Mamma said it was time to leave. Ruth wanted desperately to stay awake. Around her back, she felt the safety of the blanket and knew it was secure, for one end was tied to the baby carriage and Mamma held tightly to the other end.

Now, Ruth thought sleepily, *Mamma is the only one who must stay awake. Mamma will stay awake, and she will take care of us . . .* Her head bobbed in time to the waves under the freighter, and soon she had drifted off to sleep.

Ruth awoke to the movement of Lisa and Hannie. "Wake up, Ruth," Mamma said, settling Dieter after changing his diaper. "We are at Hela Harbor. Make sure you have your satchels, children," she reminded them.

Ruth fingered the knapsack around her neck. It was still there. Through her shirt, she could feel the coins and the paper Mamma had put inside the knapsack. The children picked up their satchels and, with the rest of the passengers, found their way off the freighter to the beach.

Here they would spend the night, waiting for a ship to arrive and take them to Denmark. Mamma looked around. There were so many people on the beach. Most of them were women and children, but a few older men who were invalids were part of the crowd.

"We will camp on the beach tonight," Mamma told the children. "Let's put our blankets here on the sand," she said.

The children settled down on the blankets. Ruth had never slept outside before. The sound of waves lapping on the beach was soothing, but it did not drown out the noise of gunfire and mortar in the distance. Here the sky was open with no protection. Ruth looked at the open sky and wondered if they would be safe tonight. *We are still in Germany, and the Allies have not stopped bombing, so how can we know we will be safe?*

Mamma helped Dieter settle in the baby carriage, moving it forward and backward in the sand. The children snuggled together on the blanket. Mamma laid down next to them. She kept her hand on the wheel of the buggy and put her head on her arm. With her other hand, she rubbed her abdomen slowly. *What is going to happen to our unborn baby?* Ruth wondered. *Is God watching over us?*

Overhead, the stars could be seen dimly through the smoke and fire in the distance. As the waves lapped gently on the shore, Ruth's body relaxed. She tried to listen for airplanes and gunfire, but sleep won out over worry as finally, finally, her eyes closed. For one last night, she would sleep on the shores of her homeland in Prussia.

In the morning, Mamma fed the children a quick breakfast so that they would be ready for the ship. All eyes scanned the horizon. Suddenly, they heard sirens. Another air raid!

"Come here, children," Mamma called. "Gather together now. Heinz, you come, too. Put your heads down here and sit close together. We will be safer if we all stay together." The children huddled next to Mamma. She held the blanket over them, and they waited.

They waited for hours, ducking their heads each time the sirens, warning of approaching Allied planes, sounded. Every time, the children shivered from fear. Each time, Mamma remained calm. Frau Noetzel and her children sat on blankets next to them, hiding under their blanket as planes flew overhead. Hundreds of other refugees waited with them. This time, there was no house or barn to run into and hide. All they had was the open beach and a blanket for cover. For now, they still had each other.

Finally, the ship pulled in and docked. Mamma shook the sand off the blanket and guided her children toward the ship. Frau Noetzel and her children and Heinz walked briskly toward the ship while Mamma followed. Bogged down by the sand, the buggy wheels moved slowly, and Mamma could not keep up.

People moved in line ahead of her, separating her from Frau Noetzel. Mamma saw that the line kept moving ahead of her, and Frau Noetzel, her children, and Heinz got onboard the big ship. Frau Noetzel stood on the deck waiting for Mamma, who was still pushing the buggy through the sand. Before Mamma could get to the gangway, the ship was full.

"There is no more room," a guard told them. He saw their looks of dismay and smiled comfortingly. "A smaller boat will come and take you to out to this ship. The water is too shallow here to load more passengers, so the ship will go out into deeper water. Once the ship is in deeper water, it can take on more passengers. You will be able to board from a smaller boat."

Mamma didn't know what to do. Yet, what else could she do?! She had carefully planned their departure, and now she was stuck at the harbor with her children because there was no room on the boat. What if the Russians came through before they could board the smaller ship and get to the larger one? What then?

Frau Noetzel, her children, and Heinz stood on the deck, waiting for Mamma and the children to join them. When Frau Noetzel noticed that Mamma was not allowed to board the ship, she got off the ship. Frau Noetzel was not going to leave Mamma alone, so they came to join Mamma.

"I am going to wait and go with you," she told Mamma. "You gave us a place to stay, and I am not going to leave you by yourself. We will wait together," she comforted Mamma.

Together, the group watched the larger ship head out to the Baltic Sea. Hopefully, they could still find passage once a smaller boat arrived to take them to the larger ship. There was nothing they could do but wait. This time, they stayed at the shore so they would be ready to get on board and not miss their turn.

After some time, a *Dampfer* [steamboat] arrived. The captain introduced himself.

"I am Captain Schlickman," he said. "My steamboat is meant for a family of seven, but we will see if we can get more on board. I will take you out to the big ship, and when we have reached water that is deep enough, the ship will be able to take more passengers."

Women and children and a few older men filed on board the boat. The captain kept asking people to keep moving to make room for more.

"*Schnell! Schnell!* [Hurry! Hurry!] Make room for more people," he kept telling those already on board, waving his hand to keep people moving while watching the sky. "It will be crowded, but it won't take long to get to the big ship, and then you will have more room."

Mamma pushed the baby buggy up the ramp and found a place onboard for the buggy. "Sit down," she told Dieter as he tried to climb out of the buggy. "Sit down, children. Make room for others," Mamma instructed. The children pushed together on the seats of the steamboat.

"Next!" the captain called, motioning to the people behind him. Mamma saw that the deck was getting full, so she ushered her children to go down below with her. By the time the steamboat was loaded, there were seventy people on board, instead of seven.

Finally, Captain Schlickman closed the gate to his family's boat. It was time to go! As the steamboat pushed off from shore, Ruth saw Mamma looking back. Mamma's eyes followed the shoreline as the steamboat moved out of port. Her face was quiet but stolid. They were leaving Danzig. They were leaving home. When would they be able to come back again?

All was quiet as the steamboat moved out to sea, heading toward the larger ship. Mothers spoke to their children in whispers as the boat headed to the ship that would take them to Denmark.

The sky shook as an airplane appeared. Another air raid! Aircraft gunfire strafed the small vessel. Passengers held their breaths. Hannie and Heinz were on one of the decks. They rushed downstairs to be with Mamma and Frau Noetzel. The silence among passengers was tense, and mothers tried to hush crying children.

Overloaded with many German refugees fleeing their homeland, the small steamboat sailed on. The waters of the Baltic sea parted as the boat glided across, heading toward the ship that would take them to a new country and a new, unknown world.

The Captain turned his steamboat west toward the larger ship ahead of them, heading to Denmark. Suddenly, a loud explosion shattered the quiet. The smaller boat rocked from the waves. Flames shot up into the sky. Ruth, her siblings, and Mamma watched from the smaller steamboat.

"A sea mine," Mamma murmured to Frau Noetzel. "Look at that boat!"

Fire shot up toward the sky as flames licked the sides of the big ship. The large ship they were going to board had hit a sea mine. All they could see now was fire.

"Thank God we were not on that boat," Mamma said.

Wide-eyed, the children watched as flames filled the sky. The hissing of steam and the roar of explosions shattered the silence of the Baltic sea. Passengers from the larger ship jumped overboard into the water and tried to swim toward the steamboat, but they never made it. Ruth saw a baby carriage floating on the water. *Is there a baby in the carriage?* she worried. Screams and cries of terror reached the German citizens in the small boat. The heat was intense as the captain moved his small boat away from the fire.

"And to think, we could have been on that ship," Frau Noetzel said to Mamma, hugging her children close.

"Yes," Mamma's eyes met Frau Noetzel's. "If the buggy wheels hadn't pushed down into the sand so I couldn't move fast enough to get to the boat, all of us might have been on that ship."

Passengers—refugees and soldiers alike—stood mesmerized as the ends of the boat came up out of the water and the middle disappeared underneath. The sounds of hissing and crackling and the stench of burning materials reminded Ruth of the night that their neighbor's barn burned. This time, they watched from a nearby steamboat instead of a frozen manure pile. Only this time, no one survived—not man or beast. Not even one.

Now they were in a predicament. What was going to happen to them?

The steamboat glided across the Baltic for a few moments while passengers watched anxiously to see where it was heading. Then Captain Schlickman made an announcement.

"I am going on to Denmark. My boat has been damaged, but we will do the best we can. I ask for your cooperation. I know your quarters are tight with so many people on board. Please try to be considerate of other passengers."

Their ship sailed on, but they were not out of danger. Enemy planes, aware that German soldiers were some of the passengers on board the ships, attempted to make attacks from the air. Sometimes they missed, but other times they hit the target. Several passengers on the boat were hit from shrapnel. Others were wounded. Some died. The dead were covered with canvases to await burial. Not only was the ship crowded with passengers; they now had to step across dead bodies when they moved on deck.

Along the Denmark shore were other boats that had provided passage from Germany. There would be many refugees needing to find a place to stay.

When their little vessel arrived at the shore, Captain Schlickman spoke. "Everybody off!" he barked to his passengers. The captain was stopped by a Danish guard.

"You cannot get out here," the guard glared. "We have too many refugees now. There is no room for any more, and I have been given orders not to allow anyone else into our country."

Silence, thick and heavy, filled the air. Nobody dared move, but they waited quietly, hopefully. Captain Schlickman stood firmly, hoping the guard would change his mind. They stood with faces of flint, staring hard at each other's eyes. Neither one of them was going to give in. The guard stood his ground, shaking his head at the captain and motioning for the Captain to get back on his steamboat. The guard didn't say another word, but his glare was enough, and Captain Schlickman's shoulders slumped as he turned to reboard his boat. The passengers on this boat would not be allowed into Denmark. They had no choice but to return.

Slowly, the captain pulled the boat back from shore. Children sat back down, and mothers dropped their heads, trying to appear unworried. It was quiet, too quiet now.

The Denmark shore was just a mirage. Their hopes faded, for this country was not a refuge after all. Even after all that they had endured and survived, there was no shelter here. Where could they go for help? There was no choice but to return to Germany.

With her siblings, Ruth sat quietly, waiting. She watched Mamma, who seemed calm as the steamboat was chartered away from the shore.

"Mamma," Lisa asked, "What will we do now?" Her lips trembled as she hugged Dieter tightly on her lap.

"Shhhh, Lisa," Mamma answered. "Sit down and be still."

The steamboat turned around with other ships that had also been refused entrance. Slowly, they headed back toward the German shore.

This time, their vessel headed toward Laboe Monument[17] near Kiel. As the harbor came into view, Hannie stood up.

"Finally," he said. "I can't wait to stand up and stretch!" He stretched his arms up over his shoulders exuberantly, bumping against others next to him.

Suddenly heavy gunfire erupted, and particles of gunfire hit the ship. Two nearby ships took a direct hit. Again, the passengers watched ships go under water as frantic occupants cried for help, jumping into the waters. Ruth and the others watched as the ships capsized, and passengers and ships went under in short order. Those not inside the cabins on Captain Schlickman's ship were also wounded. Would the burning and the killing ever stop?

There was nothing they could do, for there were no rescue ships available. To go back to Germany meant certain death. To return to Denmark guaranteed rejection. There was no place else to go. What were they to do?! Would the Baltic Sea now become their grave?

For several minutes, the ship wafted on the waters. Passengers tried to help those who were wounded. All of them waited, knowing their fate was partly in the hands of the captain. What were they going to do? What was Captain Schlickman going to do? They were indeed at his mercy.

Finally, Captain Schlickman's voice came across the loudspeaker, "I am going to take you to Denmark and leave you there. You may do what you want to, but I will take you no further. Remember, if you had been on one of those larger ships, you would have perished with those passengers. You are just fortunate to be alive on this flat-bottomed vessel."

Once again, the Captain turned his ship around and headed back to Denmark. A woman traveling with her sick father shielded him as best she could. Passengers sat hunched down, just wanting

---

[17] Laboe Naval Memorial (*a.k.a.* Laboe Tower) is a memorial located in Laboe, in Schleswig-Holstein, Germany.

the journey to be over. Idle chatter present earlier among passengers stopped. When would the waiting be over?

The smell of unwashed and dead bodies became a continual, uncomfortable odor as the steamboat sailed along. As the woman lifted the covers on her father to check on him, she discovered where the odor that bothered everyone was coming from. Her father was dead, and it was his body that smelled.

The vessel stopped at Rüegen[18] to take on some fresh water and food. Each of the refugees still had bread with them. Some had sausages to make sandwiches for the children. The cooler temperatures helped preserve the food, but the lack of water was a problem. No one could use the salty Baltic Sea water, and there was no water on board. The woman with her dead father got off the ferry at Rüegen, and the ferry continued toward Denmark.

For ten days, the refugees sat scrunched together on Captain Schlickman's ship. Their feet were swollen. They were thirsty. Mamma fed her children bread with lard on this trip because she was unable to use her burner to cook rice.

Whenever an airplane was heard, everyone scurried back inside. Dieter cried at the first sound of a plane, and Mamma scooped him up and rocked him. Mamma's arms held him securely as she rocked and rocked and rocked, his body trembling in her arms.

When will this journey ever end? Ruth wondered. *Will we ever see home again? What is Oma doing? Where is Pappa?*

Hannie and Heinz spent as much time as they could on the deck of the steamboat. The children's place to sleep was under one of the tables, and the girls and Dieter spent most of their time in the cabin off the lower deck inside the ship. It was hard to be on deck, stepping over the wounded and the dead bodies, but Hannie and Heinz didn't mind. Mamma spent most of her time in the cabin, but she allowed the children to be up and about when there was space.

---

[18] Germany's largest island, located off the Pomeranian coast in the Baltic Sea.

On the last day as the steamboat slowed its engines approaching Denmark, another air raid took place. This time, Hannie was in the cabin with Mamma, but Heinz was up on deck as their vessel became a target for the missiles. He was hit by shrapnel. Mamma and Frau Noetzel doctored Heinz's wounds as best they could, but it was evident that he needed better care, for his wounds were serious.

"Mamma, it stinks," Lisa murmured. "Everything stinks now."

"Hush, Lisa," Mamma said, wiping Heinz's forehead again. "There is nothing we can do, and it won't help the other passengers if we complain. We must be grateful that we are all alive, and we are all together."

Heinz lay listless on the floor of the cabin. Blood continued to ooze from his body and his color became paler and paler. Finally, the steamboat glided into the harbor of Gedser, Denmark. After ten days of being on the ship, what a treat it was to stand up!

"Mamma, I can hardly walk," Ruth said. "My feet are so swollen."

"My face burns," Hannie complained.

"It's from the sun and the salt water," Mamma answered. "We'll be off the boat now, so you will feel better."

The refugees waited to see what would happen when Captain Schlickman got off the boat this time. With his face stern and unrelenting, the captain got off his ship and spoke to the guard who glared at him.

"I cannot take these people back to Germany," Captain Schlickman said, shaking his finger in the guard's face. "I've been shot at! My boat has holes in it and I have engine trouble! To take them back to Germany means certain death. Please have mercy on their souls!"

The port authority was not too happy to see them again. He stood, glaring at the Captain, shaking his head.

"I can't take them anywhere else," Captain Schlickman insisted. "I am having engine problems now, and this ship can't make another passage." He stood taller now, his face and demeanor demanding respect and daring the guard to deny the passengers entrance.

The guards looked at the Captain and his ship. Did he see the women and children peering at them from the ship? Would he have pity on them? Several of the guards huddled together, conferring.

Finally, one of the guards spoke.

"Bring them in," he told the Captain. Then shaking his finger in Captain Schlickman's face, he shouted, "But don't you dare bring us any more than this shipload!"

"I couldn't even if I wanted to," Captain Schlickman replied. "This ship needs work before it can sail again."

The guard nodded reluctantly. "Bring them in," he said.

Sighs of relief—and trepidation—filled the air.

Mamma stood up, holding Dieter on her hip. She stumbled as she took a step forward. Her feet were so swollen that it was hard to move. Ruth, Lisa, and Hannie tried to move their feet, but it was difficult. For ten days, they sat with little to eat or to drink. The swelling in their feet and paralysis from numbness made it difficult to walk. Mamma put Dieter into the baby carriage and arranged their belongings.

"This way!" the captain called. "Come this way! Make room, make room. Everyone who is well needs to get off first!"

The refugees looked at each other dubiously. Had they really arrived safely? Slowly, they picked their way across those who were wounded. Averting their eyes, they moved past the tarp-covered bodies and found their way off the ship.

Mamma tried to hurry the children along, putting her hands on the sides of their heads, encouraging them to look straight ahead. The stench was unbearable, but soon they would be off the ship. Those who could walk led the way off the ship. Next, the wounded would be removed. When all living passengers were off the boat, soldiers would carry the dead onto the shore. Guards stood watching the passengers as they stumbled down the gangplank.

As Mamma made her way toward the exit, she talked to one of the soldiers about Heinz, who by now could hardly talk.

"He will need to go to the hospital," the soldier told her. "We will see to it that he gets to the hospital."

Mamma was sorry to leave Heinz, but she knew it had to be done. Hannie was sad to leave his buddy, but there was no time to lose. It was time to get off the boat. [It was also too soon to know that they would never see their young friend Heinz again.]

Not only was the stench from dead bodies unbearable, but passengers reeked of sweat, vomit, and diarrhea. No one had been able to bathe during the ten-day journey. The air was filled with salt water, fish odors, and the smell of cattle.

Nearby was a long, flat, tin-roofed cattle shed that had been used as a holding shed before Denmark's poultry and cattle were shipped out of the country. The cattle shed had once been empty, but now it was used for German soldiers and other refugees.

It was May 10, 1945, and they were safe in Denmark. They had survived the steamboat ride to Denmark and, except for Pappa, they were all together. The cattle shed would be their home for the night.

~ Chapter Five ~

A Place in a Denmark Cattle Shed

May 10-11, 1945

The long line of refugees moved slowly. No matter how old or how young, walking was very difficult. Older people who had hardly moved for days crept along the gangplank, shuffling their feet. Even children struggled to walk evenly. Everyone's feet were swollen. The haggard refugees, most of them women and children, gathered on the shore.

Danish guards on shore directed the refugees as the lines moved forward, and soon the group found themselves inside the cattle shed. Even though the floors had been swept, they seemed dirty. Light filtered in through the cracks in the empty shed. Splintery walls promised protection from wind for the night, but nothing more. There was no place else to go. This was Denmark, and the cattle shed is where Ruth and her family would spend their first night.

Mamma looked around, trying to decide where to put her things and her children. Dieter and Ruth were sick and weak from diarrhea. Their clothing was disheveled and dirty. Some of their clothes were too dirty to be cleaned; yet they had so few items with them. What to do?! There was no water in the shed, and only straw ticks for bedding were tossed onto the floor.

"How are eight of us going to sleep on these two straw ticks?" Mamma murmured to Frau Noetzel.

Together, they spread the straw ticks on the floor and started to unpack.

"At least we are not on the boat fearing for our lives," Frau Noetzel encouraged, shaking out a blanket she had used on the steamboat.

Mamma nodded, "You are right, and we can be thankful for that!"

"Can I go outside and see what this place is like, Mamma?" Hannie begged.

Mamma nodded. "You can go look. See if you can find any bathrooms or water."

She caught Dieter as he tried to climb out of the buggy. "You can get down and walk now, son," she said. "Come, children, let's take our shoes off and stretch!"

Getting boots and shoes off was not an easy task either. It was hard to bend over because their muscles were so stiff.

"Mamma, I can't get my boots off," Ruth complained, pulling at the heel of her boot. "My feet hurt."

"That's because they are swollen," Mamma replied.

She bent over, pulling gently at Ruth's boots to remove them from her feet. Lisa managed to get her own boots off. Mamma stood up, stretching and rubbing her lower back. Her abdomen was getting larger as the baby inside her grew, and bending over was not becoming easier.

"Mamma, there are water troughs out here," Hannie called as he came back inside. "We could wash up there."

"Let's go, children," Mamma said eagerly. "Any water is better than no water."

They trudged over to the water trough and attempted to wash off ten days' accumulation of dirt, sweat, colds, diarrhea, and runny noses. Even though the water wasn't warm, it felt good to be free of the grime from their journey.

"Let's get some water to cook with," Mamma said. She filled her kettle with water from a faucet at the other end of the stable, They then returned to their corner in the cattle shed. Mamma cooked rice with the alcohol burner she had brought along. The rice meal was their first meal in Denmark.

"Do you children know what today is?," Mamma asked them as they finished supper.

"How can anybody know what today is?," Lisa complained. "We have been on the boat for so long."

"Today is May 10. It is Dieter's birthday! Happy birthday, *mein Sohn* [my son!"]. Mamma smiled tenderly at Dieter.

"Happy Birthday, Dieter!" the children chorused together. Dieter smiled bashfully and hid his face.

"I wish Pappa were here," Hannie said wistfully.

"Me, too," Lisa murmured.

"And we don't have any birthday present for Dieter," Ruth said sadly.

"Dieter is too little to understand," Mamma smiled at her children. "We are together, and we are safe. Being safe is the best birthday present he could have, don't you think?"

Dieter's siblings nodded. They were safe, at least for now.

"Come, children," Mamma attempted cheerfulness. "You can go play outside for a while."

Ruth, Hannie, Lisa, and Frau Noetzel's children ran outside to play. There were many other children to play with, and for a few minutes, they forgot their days at sea and the fear of death. Never mind the smell of the stables. Never mind how dirty everything seemed. For now, they could move about and not feel cramped and stifled.

At long last, the fear of sirens shattering the calm was gone. No more fear of air raids destroying property and lives. For now, they were safe. After the children tired of playing outside, they found Mamma in the cattle shed. Dieter was already asleep in his buggy.

"Let's put your coats on the straw tick," Mamma suggested. "It will help make your beds more comfortable while you sleep."

Soon all of them piled onto the straw tick.

"Stop wiggling!" Lisa told Hannie.

"I can't help it. I can't get comfortable!," Hannie replied, kicking his feet on the tick.

"Hush, children," Mamma admonished. "Try to be still and rest. We don't want Dieter to wake up, and we must not keep other people awake. We need to rest for tomorrow."

"What happens tomorrow, Mamma?" Ruth asked.

"We will see. Tonight, we sleep, and tomorrow we will see," Mamma replied.

Will we be home before the baby comes? Ruth wondered. *Where will we go from here? Where is Pappa? Will we ever see him again? How long will we stay here? When can we go back home?*

Ruth closed her eyes and tried not to think about the long boat ride. She tried to forget the airplanes in the sky, roaring overhead and dropping bombs around them. With her eyes closed, she could still almost feel the rocking of the steamboat. Ruth tried to block out the sight of other ships sinking into the murky waters and passengers jumping overboard. She tried to forget about the sight of dead bodies covered with tarps when they walked off the ship. Could she ever forget the smell of the old man who died when no one even knew until his body started to stink? She tried not to worry about Heinz. *Who are these people in Denmark who allowed us to enter their county? Where will we go tomorrow? Where is Pappa? Is he safe?*

Slowly, slowly, Ruth's eyes closed. The wiggling of Hannie's feet had almost stopped. She heard the gentle breathing of Dieter. Beside her, Lisa slept soundly. Mamma turned on one side, then the other. It must be hard for Mamma to have to sleep on the floor. *How soon will the baby come?* Ruth wondered. It had been two years since Dieter was born. *Will Dieter even remember our home in Prussia,* she wondered, *when we get back home? Will we ever be able to go back home?*

Home. It seemed so far away. It was far away. They were in a new country now. When will we be able to go back? Will we ever go back?

Ruth's eyes felt heavy. Mamma wasn't turning from one side

to the other anymore. She must be asleep, too. *Home*, Ruth decided, *is where we are all together.*

At least we are all together, she thought. *All of us, that is, but Pappa.* With those thoughts in her heart, Ruth drifted off to sleep.

During the night while the Reimer children slept, German soldiers freely molested women and older girls who had fled their homeland.[19] These despicable, immoral acts were performed in the presence of other children without any shame. Mamma was aware of what was happening, but there was nothing she could do but pray. The soldiers did not bother her or her children. Frau Noetzel and her children were safe as well. As Mamma lay awake that night, she was grateful they had made it to Denmark safely. Yet, she couldn't help but wonder: *what was ahead of her and her family? What was going to happen to them now?*

---

[19] Gingerich, p. 34.

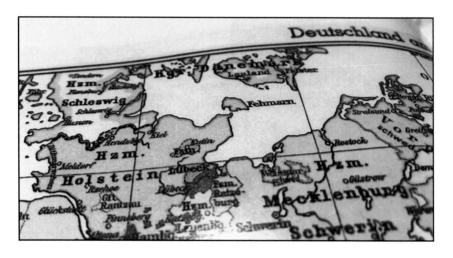

An older map of the Baltic Sea and Germany.

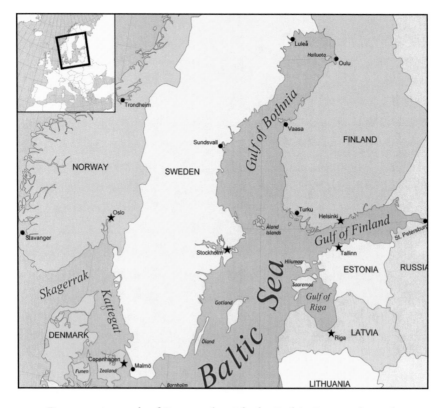

Germany is south of Denmark with the Baltic Sea on the right.

~ Chapter Six ~

A PLACE IN CAMP GEDSER

HALB INSEL [HALF ISLAND OR PENINSULA]

May 11, 1945 - October 1945

Ruth opened her eyes and tried to remember where she was. Sunlight shone through the cracks of the walls. Then she remembered. They were in Denmark, in the cattle shed. Sounds of children crying, mothers' soothing voices, and older children outside at play woke the Reimer children.

For breakfast, Mamma once again cooked rice. Soon after breakfast, a large truck lumbered into the camp. Then another truck came, and another one.

Across the loudspeaker came an announcement:

"*Bekannt Machung!* [Announcement!] Today, you will be taken to Camp Gedser.[20] This is a camp for *Flüchtlinge* [refugees]. Please gather all your belongings and get ready to be moved to the new location."

The voice continued triumphantly:

"To be sure everyone is aware, we give you this news: Germany *ergibt sich* [has surrendered] to the Allies! The treaty of surrender was signed on the 8th of May."

Refugees stood at attention and listened to the announcement. At the mention that the war was over, there was little reaction. Just silence as each pondered what this meant. No cheers, no tears, no hurrahs! The war was over, but they were not free. What the announcer did not say, but what Mamma realized, was that now they

---

[20] Gedser is a small port town on the island of Falster and is the southernmost town in Denmark.

were civilian prisoners of war. Did this mean those German soldiers would become prisoners along with them?!

Lisa and Hannie helped Mamma get the baby carriage onto the truck. Mamma checked each child to make sure the knapsacks were still around their necks. Clutching their satchels, Ruth and Lisa followed Mamma. The plates and cups Ruth and Lisa had packed from home were nestled safely inside their satchels.

"Mamma," Hannie said, "Aren't you going to take the stove?"

Mamma turned and looked at the stove. She shook her head. "No, I am going to leave it here. I don't have any fuel left to use for cooking, and hopefully the camp they are taking us to will provide food for us."

Dieter clung to Mamma as they climbed on board the truck with other refugees. Frau Noetzel, Renate, and Marianne followed them onto the truck.

Ruth wondered about Heinz. *Did he make it to the hospital? Is he feeling better? Will we ever see him again?* Her reverie was broken as the refugees pushed together as closely as they could to make room for more people.

It feels like we are a bunch of animals, Ruth thought. *Just like a bunch of animals who don't get to choose where they go or what happens to them.*

The drive to the new camp did not take long because it was just a few miles from the cattle shed. Before long the crowded trucks pulled into the new camp. The drivers came around to open the back of the trucks. Carefully, the refugees climbed down from the trucks. Ruth looked around at the many buildings, so many long, long buildings. Everything was strange.

"You will find a place inside these barracks," the driver told them. "These barracks have been set up for German refugees. There are many of you, and there are plenty of places in these barracks. *Kommen sie!* [Come!] Get off the truck and find a place!" he urged them.

The guard seemed to feel good about the place that was

provided for them. To Ruth, the barracks appeared foreboding, distant, and cold. This was not like home. No pretty flowers, no vegetables in a garden for fresh produce, no furrowed fields stretching for acres across farmlands. No stately house with a yard in which children could play. No trees providing shade for girls to play with dolls on a warm summer day. Just long stretches of buildings called *Barracken* [Barracks].

Mamma and the children unloaded the baby carriage, picked up their satchels, and followed Frau Noetzel and her children and the long line of refugees along the row of barracks. Finally, they found a barrack with plenty of room. The barracks were large rooms with straw ticks on the floor for sleeping. No tables, no chairs, and no beds.

There was room for 70 people in each barrack. This barrack looked like it had once been used, but now it was abandoned.

"This was a soldiers' camp," one of the Danish guards explained. "You will pick up your meals in the kitchen every day. There is plenty of tea, but there is not much food."

"It's good we will have some food here," Mamma murmured quietly to the children. "Since I don't have any more rice or bread with lard."

"We need to unpack our things," Lisa said. "Once we have our plates and cups unpacked, it will feel more like home."

Ruth nodded. Together, the girls unwrapped the plates they had brought from home. They would need these when it was time to go through the food line for meals.

What Mamma didn't know was that their food would consist of one piece of bread for breakfast and another piece for supper, and one dipper of soup for lunch.

"This isn't soup!" Hannie said disgustedly as he tasted his first serving of soup that day at lunch.

"It has some nutrients in it, and eating it will help us stay healthy," Mamma responded.

"It's just some dried vegetables in broth," Hannie replied.

"It is food, and it is nutrition for us," Mamma answered. "We will be grateful for what we have to eat."

Resourceful as always, Mamma used the abundant warm tea to wash her children's faces and bodies as best she could. The warm tea would have to do, since there was no warm water.

Now that the war was over, the German refugees were civilian prisoners. In the next days, guards constructed a barbed wire fence around the perimeter of the camp, a fence to prevent anyone from trying to make an escape. The guards carried guns on their backs and watched the prisoners to make certain none of them would try to go past the perimeter. German soldiers were also prisoners of war; they were loaded onto trucks and taken away. As Mamma watched the prisoners loaded up into the truck to be driven away, she felt relief. These soldiers were to have been their protectors; instead, once they arrived on Denmark's shore, they abused those least able to defend themselves. It made her sad and angry at the same time. Her face was resolute, and Ruth knew Mamma was going to try her hardest to make sure her family was safe.

Mamma and the children were grateful they had a place to stay. The conditions were poor, but they were safe. There was not much food, and diseases and insects plagued the refugees, but they were safe. There were no air raids, no bombs dropped, and no German soldiers taking advantage of them. They were all together and no one had been hurt.

Back home on the farm in West Prussia, there had always been much to do. Mamma had her housework and later farmwork when Pappa was gone. The children had places to play and toys with which to play. Here, there was no housekeeping or farming for Mamma except to keep her area of the barrack clean and to watch over her children, trying to keep them as healthy as possible. Here, there were no toys or games for children to play, but they had plenty of playmates who helped devise things to do. During the daylight hours, children played outside. Softballs made from rags filled with newspaper worked well and provided hours of entertainment—

until the newspapers disintegrated from being hit so often. With so many children, there were plenty of ideas for improvising games and fun things to do. Even though this was not home, it was easier to forget about the conditions in which they lived with so many playmates to occupy their time. They didn't mind getting dirty or having so little because everyone else in the camp was as impoverished as they were.

Mealtimes, once a highlight of the day, were not appealing. The single slice of bread given for their meal was a dark sourdough bread, so different from what was familiar to them. The refugees' diet had changed drastically in just a few weeks' time, and many of them developed intestinal problems. Young children had a harder time digesting the unfamiliar sourdough bread, and some of them developed fever and diarrhea.

Dieter was one of those children. Alas, Mamma's care in keeping her children clean and parceling some of her food to them did not keep Dieter from getting sicker. Ruth knew Mamma was trying hard to keep Dieter clean, even with his constant diarrhea.

"This place is so dirty that I don't know what to do," Mamma told Lisa one day. "We must keep our bodies clean, even if the barrack is not clean. If we can stay clean, we will be healthier."

"Yet Dieter is still sick, Mamma," Lisa answered. "What are we going to do?"

"I know, Lisa," Mamma murmured as she changed Dieter again. "He is becoming weaker. He doesn't have the food he needs for his little body, and his diarrhea is worse. I am afraid he will become dehydrated."

"Maybe you should take him to the clinic," Lisa worried.

"I don't have money for a hospital or for doctors," Mamma's voice was sad. "We need to pray that he will get better."

A few days later Dieter woke up with his body feverish and his face flushed. "Oh Dieter," Mamma said, "I think I had better take you to the clinic."

At the clinic, the nurses encouraged Mamma to give the listless toddler more liquids—more tea—to help keep his fever down. Nothing Mamma did helped Dieter get better. Instead, he became weaker and paler. Finally, it was decided he needed to go to the hospital.

"I don't have money to pay for the hospital," Mamma wrung her hands together.

"Our government will not charge you for his care, Frau Reimer," a nurse assured her. A guard accompanied Mamma to the hospital where Dieter was admitted. Mamma was not allowed to stay, so she left her little boy in the care of the Danish people. It was hard to leave her son, but she had no choice. The guard accompanied Mamma back to the camp where the children were waiting for her.

"They said they will keep Dieter for a few days," Mamma said wearily. "He is so weak. Not only does he have diarrhea, he has a bad case of lice."

The hospital was too far away for Mamma to visit Dieter every day. In addition, a guard needed to accompany her, so she could not come and go as she longed to do. Every day, Mamma reminded her children to pray for Dieter.

In the meantime, another child in the camp became ill with a high fever, caused by an infection in her ear. When the fever was gone, the child could no longer hear. Mothers rocked their crying children, hoping they would recover from their illnesses. Many of them didn't. There were thousands of children in the camps, and few under the age of three survived. Refugee camp living was difficult. There were more people than food. More sicknesses than medicine. More sadness than smiles. More hunger than health. More filth than soap, and more death than life.

After a few weeks in the hospital, Dieter was able to come home. A guard accompanied Mamma to the hospital and back to the refugee camp. Dieter's head rested on Mamma's shoulder and he lay quietly in her arms as she trudged back from the hospital.

"What happened to his hair?!" Ruth asked when Mamma arrived back in the barrack.

"They had to shave his head because of the lice. Don't worry, Ruth. His hair will grow back. Now we just need to help our boy get stronger."

The good medical care and nutritious food in the Danish hospital had helped Dieter recover. Even so, by the time his hospital stay was over, he was too weak to stand and or walk by himself. Mamma spent time each day helping him stand on his feet and learn to walk again. Lisa and Ruth took turns helping by holding his hands and walking with him as he tottered along.

Dieter did not forget the good food he was served in the hospital, and he was too young to understand why there was no food like that for him in the camp! He didn't want the food in the refugee camp. He wanted something better, and he let Mamma know!

Every morning, Dieter begged, *"Ich will weitel brot mit butter und zucker, Mamma. Ich will weitel brot mit butter und zucker!"* [I want white bread with butter and sugar, Mamma. I want white bread with butter and sugar!] Each morning, Mamma's face grew sad. How she wished she could give her little boy what he so desperately wanted and needed! Mamma had no butter and she had no sugar. All Mamma could give him was his daily share of one piece of dark sourdough bread for breakfast and another for supper, and soup for lunch.

More than once, Ruth watched Mamma try to blink away tears when Dieter begged for *brot mit butter und zucker*. Ruth wondered when they would have bread with butter and sugar again. *Is there ever going to be a time when there is good food and we won't be hungry?* she asked herself.

Every day, children in the camp received immunizations. Whooping cough and diphtheria were prevalent, and nurses made the rounds each day, immunizing more children to prevent the spread of childhood diseases that might take even more lives. There were hundreds of children, so it took many weeks to immunize every child in the camp. Several times a week, the children were given cod liver oil, a brownish yellow liquid taken by teaspoonsful.

"I don't like this cod liver oil," Ruth complained to Mamma. "It doesn't taste like what you used to give us at home."

"I know, Ruth," Mamma soothed. "But it will help you keep from getting sick. We need to do everything we can to stay healthy. Dieter has already been sick; I don't need any more of my children getting sick. Please take it, and don't complain."

Lice, fleas, and bedbugs were also prevalent in the camp. Mamma did her best to keep her children clean, but it was difficult to do without plenty of soap and water. In addition, living in quarters with over 70 people in one long barrack only heightened the spread of disease and infections. Mamma knew this camp was a smaller camp than others and had only hundreds of refugees, and she was grateful.

Every day, the itching worsened. Bedbugs crawled into the straw ticks and came out at night, feasting on blood from the sleeping children.

When it was time to wash hair, Mamma used kerosene.

"It smells!" Ruth exclaimed, squinting her eyes.

"I know it doesn't smell good, but it will help get rid of the lice in your hair," Mamma was firm.

The first blankets given to the refugees were paper blankets. Lying on their straw tick beds at night, the children could hear fleas landing on the paper blankets.

"At least we can hear the fleas," Hannie said. "If I were a soldier, I'd be able to find the fleas when they jumped on the paper blankets. I guess that's one good thing about having paper blankets," he laughed, "even though the blankets always want to slide off of you."

In time, the paper blankets were exchanged for regular blankets. After that, it was harder to hear the bugs landing on the blankets. Nevertheless, the children continued to fight the insects, for each one killed was one less to make their lives miserable.

Mealtimes did not provide ample nourishment for the refugees. Long lines formed up to the kitchen window with each person carrying his own tin bowl and cup. At the window, food was rationed to the refugees. At times, young children were given rations of milk. Mamma was grateful for rye coffee even though there was no sugar to be added. Occasionally, cream of wheat was served for lunch instead of soup. Mamma and the children learned that waiting until the cream of wheat was cold made it easier to beat. Mamma got the idea to let it get cold instead of eating it right away. Once it was cold, they could beat it until it became fluffy like whipped cream. Beating the cream of wheat made it much richer, smoother, and easier to eat and digest.

One day Mamma found someone who was willing to trade clothing for food. She traded two of the nightgowns she had brought for her girls in exchange for food for her children.

When the children's shoes wore out or no longer fit, they made their own footwear. Feet were traced on a board, then the board was cut into the shape of the foot. Straps were applied using discarded, worn-out shoelaces from soldiers. [Today, this footwear would be called flip flops, but then they considered them shoes.]

Although the family had few choices of clothing, Mamma knew there was one thing she could do: keep the clothing clean. When it was time to do laundry, Mamma enlisted the help of her children.

"I know this place is not especially clean, but we will do the best we can to keep ourselves and our clothes clean," Mamma told the children. "It is one way we can stay healthier. Help me carry our clothing to the tubs."

The children helped carry their dirty clothing to the washing facilities. There they soaked the clothing in buckets and then washed them in huge tubs. After that, Mamma and the children wrung out the clothes and took them back to the barrack. Inside the barrack, the laundry was thrown across lines strung across the room.

Toilets were close to the washrooms. These toilets were like one large outhouse with as many as 10-20 seat holes crudely fashioned for use. Male and female toilets were in the same building, with a large dividing wall separating the men's from the ladies' toilets. By now, the family grasped that the war was over. Germany had lost the war. Hitler was dead. Nobody knew if Pappa had survived or if he was in a prison camp somewhere. German soldiers who had occupied Denmark were now prisoners of the Danish, and the Danes were taking revenge on the soldiers who had invaded their country. They also ridiculed the refugees whom they had been sent to guard.

As the women and children walked past the guardhouses on their way to the wash houses, the Danish guards delighted in calling out *"Tishke Schweinhund!"* [German pig-dogs!][21]

"When you hear the soldiers make fun of you, just keep on walking," Mamma told her children. "Look straight ahead. If you try to talk back to them, you might get a beating, or they might not let you eat your meals that day. Just ignore them."

This was hard for the children to do. They had no choice but to be here in this camp. They had no choice in who the guards were or what they said to them. Ruth's face burned with shame, but she kept her eyes straight ahead while walking past the guardhouse. She felt like yelling back, but she remembered what Mamma had said, so she kept on walking. Talking back might bring beatings or reduce food rations, and she did not want any harm to come to her or her siblings.

Each barrack housed 70 refugees, most of whom were women and children. Illness and disease continued to be rampant, and the ravages of war were keenly felt. As innocent children succumbed to disease, grief was a constant. Each day brought sadness as families lost

---

[21] Gingerich, p. 35.

one child after another to the devastation from disease. Mothers who had worked hard to take care of their children cried long into the night, wishing there was something more they could have done. Little graves were dug at the edge of the camp in a burial ground, and soldiers helped mothers bury their little ones. Elderly people too frail to withstand the onslaught of illness and disease also perished. As both old and young were buried, their clothing was passed on to others.

Away from home and other family members, the refugees forged bonds with others. They made new friends, and some even found distant relatives. Relatives who hardly knew each other before the war found comfort in finding distant family members and connecting with them. In this camp, Mamma found three sisters who were her distant cousins. The children had never met these distant cousins before, but Mamma was comforted in having family near her, even though they didn't know each other well.

Being together in the same camp and having no one else to call family brought kinship and comradery. One of the three cousins, Liesbet Bench, came to the barrack one day in August to check on Mamma.

"How are you feeling today, Gerda?" Liesbet asked when she saw Mamma pacing the floor, taking slow, deep breaths.

"I think it is time for the baby to come," Mamma told Liesbet as her children listened.

"I can go with you to the clinic if you would like," Liesbet offered. Mamma nodded.

"Lisa, you will need to look after the children," Mamma stopped pacing to look at her oldest daughter.

"I can take care of them," Lisa replied stoutly, trying not to be worried.

"I'll help, too," Hannie replied.

Before long, Mamma and Liesbet left to walk to the clinic. There, after many hours of labor, little Heidi was born. It was August 13, 1945, three and a half months since they left West Prussia. Liesbet came back to the barrack to tell the children that their sister had been born, then she went back to help take care of Mamma.

While Mamma was in the clinic, twelve-year-old Lisa was responsible to look after her younger siblings. There were other mothers in the camp who knew that Mamma was gone, and they kept a watchful eye on the children as well. By this time, the barrack had become home to Ruth, and having Lisa in charge because Mamma was gone was not frightening.

This was the second time Mamma gave birth to a child without Pappa. The first time was in 1943 when Dieter was born in Tiegenhof. Pappa had been in the Nazi army then, and travel was unsafe. The midwife was six kilometers away and none of the workers wanted to risk their lives to bring her to the farm. Some of the workers were prisoners of war, so it was not safe to send them for the midwife. Instead of having her baby at home, Mamma decided to go to the hospital and found a friend to take her. That time, even though Pappa wasn't there, the family knew he was alive. This time, although there was joy at the birth of a baby girl, there was also sadness. Mamma did not have much milk for the baby, and Pappa didn't even know that there was going to be a baby. Now he might never learn to know his daughter.

Is Pappa still alive? Ruth wondered. *Will he ever know about Heidi?*

A few days after the birth of the new baby, Mamma came back from the clinic. In her arms was a tiny bundle. The children crowded around to see their new sister.

"She's so tiny," Lisa whispered. "Can I hold her?"

"Yes, you can hold her," Mamma smiled tiredly.

Each child had a turn holding the new baby. What fun it was to hold their little sister! They were careful with Heidi and were grateful for the joy of a new sibling in spite the chaos of living in a refugee camp. Having a new sibling to love brought simple pleasure to the entire family.

When Mamma came back to the barracks with her new baby, she carried a yellow paper in her hands. The lined yellow paper was Heidi's birth certificate, complete with her name, the date of her birth, and the name of the clinic in Denmark. [This certificate became the only birth certificate Mamma had for any of her children, for the others were all lost due to the war.]

The newborn was a fussy baby. Because Heidi was always hungry, she was not content. Heidi did not get enough nutrition because she didn't get a lot of milk. It wasn't long until Heidi developed sores on her body, and Mamma took her to the clinic. There the nurses lanced her sores and then bathed and dressed her. Sometimes they washed her body in a blue liquid.

Heidi's clothing and blankets were pieces left over from other clothing too small or too worn to be used by anyone else. Even though Heidi's clothes were remnants of others' clothing, Mamma worked hard to keep them clean.

"I think her sores seem to be healed, Mamma," Lisa said one day as she wrapped her sister in the clean rags Mamma had prepared. "Yes, but her stomach is not better. She is having diarrhea, and I am afraid she is going to become dehydrated," Mamma worried.

Heidi wasn't growing as a newborn should, and she continued to be fussy. Her mouth rooted for food and nourishment, but there was so little to give. Even though the sores seemed to be better, they didn't go away. Lisa and Ruth took turns holding her to help Mamma.

Finally, one day, Mamma took Heidi back to the clinic. The nurses decided that she needed to go to the hospital. Once again, Mamma was at the mercy of the Danish government. She had no money to pay for her child's care, yet they admitted her anyway.

Mamma had permission to visit Heidi every week. A guard had to accompany her, and the children had to stay at the camp. When Mamma went to the hospital, she left Lisa in charge of her other children. On her day to visit the hospital, she was gone most of the afternoon and was tired when she got back. The only transportation she had was to walk to and from the hospital. Each week, she came home and gave her children an update. Each time, she asked the children to pray.

"We must pray for your baby sister every day," Mamma told them over and over. Her face was sad and serious. Mamma was so thin. *I know Mamma is worried because Heidi doesn't get enough milk,* Ruth thought.

One day when Mamma went to the hospital to see Heidi, she learned that Heidi had turned blue and was able to sip only a little bit of tea. The doctor spoke with Mamma privately.

"I am afraid your little one is not going to make it, Frau Reimer," the doctor's voice was kind. "We will have to wait and see, but you must prepare yourself. When you come back next week, she might not be alive, or she could be better. *Es tut mir so leid.* [I am so sorry.]"

When Mamma came back to the barracks that day, she gathered her children together. "Heidi is very, very sick," Mamma's voice trembled and there were tears in her eyes. "We must pray for her. I don't know if she will get better. The doctor told me today that he is not sure she will live."

"Oh Mamma," Lisa's eyes were teary. "I want Heidi to live! Pappa doesn't even know about her. She has to live!"

Ruth's lip quivered. Hannie ground his fist into his eyes and looked away.

"We will pray for Heidi, and we will trust God to take care of her," Mamma answered.

There was nothing else to do but to pray and to trust God. Every day, they prayed for little Heidi. They hoped the care she was getting from the Danish people in their hospital would help her get better.

Mamma returned to the hospital the following week. The children watched her leave with the guard and wondered what news she would have when she returned. What would Mamma find when she got to the hospital?! It was a long afternoon. Lisa watched Dieter while Hannie and Ruth played outside with the other children in the camp. It seemed that Mamma was taking a long time to come back.

Finally, they saw her walking through the camp. She walked briskly and didn't look upset. When Mamma got closer, Ruth noticed at once that the worry lines on her face were gone. She was smiling! The children ran to meet her.

"Did you see Heidi?," Hannie asked breathlessly. "Is she better?"

"Yes, children," Mamma's eyes shone. "Heidi is better. The doctor said she can probably come home next week!"

"Oh Mamma!," Lisa exclaimed. "I was so worried. This is such good news! God answered our prayers!"

"Yes, children," Mamma was beaming, and she didn't look tired anymore. "God has answered our prayers."

Day in and day out, life in the camp remained the same. The menu had little variety: bread for breakfast and supper, soup or occasionally cream of wheat soup for lunch. Immunizations continued to be given by the nurses. Hundreds of babies were born, but just as many children died. The graveyard at the edge of the camp became larger as more graves were dug and filled. Bedbugs and lice continued to be a problem. Stomachs always felt empty, and it was hard to remember what it felt like to not be hungry.

Then Lisa became ill. Mamma tried to nurse her, but she wasn't getting better.

"Mamma, I don't feel good," Lisa whimpered one morning. Mamma knew if Lisa complained, she was sick. "Let's walk over to the clinic," Mamma urged Lisa.

"I don't feel good enough to walk over there," Lisa said. "I'm so tired."

"I'll help you, Lisa," Mamma said. She looked at Ruth. "You stay here with the children and watch them for me. I shouldn't be gone long."

Ruth nodded. It made her feel important to have Mamma put her in charge. Usually Lisa was the one Mamma left in charge. But this time, Lisa was the one who was sick.

"I'll watch them," Ruth assured Mamma.

"And I will help Ruth watch Dieter," Hannie assured his mother. Mamma helped Lisa get out of bed and put her arm around her as they walked out of the barrack. Lisa was bent over, and her face was pale. Mamma kept her arm tightly around Lisa and soon they arrived in the clinic.

The nurses in the clinic didn't know how to help Lisa anymore, so it was decided that she needed to go to the hospital. There, Lisa received more food and nourishment and was able to recover. Before long, she was back at the camp with Mamma and the other children.

Mamma hoped to hear about Pappa sometime, but she wasn't sure how to get in touch with him. She knew she could write to Oma Hintz or Oma Reimer, but that took paper and stamps. Little did she know that she would be able to find a way soon, and it was through Mennonite Central Committee (MCC).[22]

One day Mamma was told to come to the office to get supplies. She walked to the office to find out what supplies they were giving her. They told her that care packages had come from America for refugees. Mamma was one of the first refugees to receive a package. The person in the office gave her a package and told her it was hers to keep. What could it be? Mamma walked briskly when she left the office, carrying her package. She was so excited that she felt like running, but she hurried as fast as she could. Mamma could hardly wait to get back to the barrack to her children so she could open her package. Camp personnel told her that items had come from Mennonite people in America who wanted to help the refugees, particularly Mennonite refugees.

---

[22] A worldwide ministry of Anabaptist churches founded in 1920. See Appendix B.

When she came back to the barrack, she called her children to come inside. From the sound of her voice, they knew she had something important to tell them, so they came running.

Mamma's face glowed with excitement. On the package was a label, "In the Name of Christ," stamped MCC (Mennonite Central Committee). Mamma opened the package and pulled out a brand-new blanket. For a few moments, Mamma and the children stood, looking at the blanket. It was pretty and soft, and it was brand new! The blanket was clean and would provide warmth. Mamma ran her hands over the softness. Gingerly, Lisa and Ruth reached out and touched its edges, reveling in its fluffiness. Mamma picked up her suitcase with her sewing supplies and opened it up. She reached inside, took out her scissors, and spread the blanket out on her straw tick bed.

 In the name of Christ

As Mamma picked up the scissors and started cutting, her children gasped.

"What are you doing, Mamma?!" Ruth exclaimed.

"I am making blankets for our baby," Mamma's face glowed. "Now our little Heidi will have some nice, clean blankets to keep her warm."

Seeing Mamma smile brought joy to her children. Ruth, Hannie, and Lisa looked at Mamma and then smiled at each other. How long had it been since they had seen Mamma smile?! Now Heidi would have something soft and new for a blanket instead of old, frayed rags. It was almost too good to be true.

"Now you won't need to tear other things apart to make a blanket for Heidi," Lisa smiled happily, fingering the fabric. "It's so clean and soft."

As Mamma wrapped Heidi in her new, soft blanket, Ruth wondered about the people who had sent the blanket. Who were they? She didn't know, and Mamma didn't know. She knew that this blanket had made Mamma smile, and she felt warm inside. *God bless those people, whoever they are,* she thought.

Between April and October, Mamma and the children had left their homeland and traveled to Denmark. They had celebrated the arrival of a new baby. Three of Mamma's five children had been hospitalized. Now they were all together again. The war was over, but they still did not know where Pappa was or even if he was still alive. Yet Mamma, Ruth knew, was grateful. The graveyard that held many children at the edge of the camp did not hold any of Mamma's children. Each evening, they were all together, safe in their barrack. Would it always be so? Only God knew.

Chapter Seven

A Place in Camp Hasselö

November 1945 - May 1947

One morning the guards announced that the refugees would be moving to another camp. Camp Gedser was being closed, so refugees were being moved to other camps. With some trepidation, Mamma and the children gathered their few belongings and boarded the trucks with other refugees. Would this place be cleaner and smaller, or would it be even dirtier and larger?

The drive took some time, and then the truck turned into the new barracks. This was Camp Hasselö.[23] The barracks here were smaller than the ones in Camp Gedser. These barracks were referred to as Sweden barracks because they were brought in from Sweden. Because they were wooden, the pieces could be taken apart for transport and then set back up in the camp. Mamma and the children entered the building to which they were assigned.

"Look, Mamma, a table and benches!," Lisa exclaimed.

"It's not as big, so it won't be as crowded," Hannie added.

"And we won't need to sit on the floor to eat," Ruth smiled happily.

Mamma smiled, too. "Yes, children, this place is not as crowded; we will have more room. Let's get our things unpacked and get settled."

It didn't take long to unpack because they didn't own much. Blankets, some utensils, and meager clothing. Ruth and Lisa were happy to unpack the plates and cups they had brought from home. Getting settled in brought a semblance of order in the chaotic refugee

---

[23] Hasselö Plantage is a coastal village located on the Danish island of Falster.

barrack. Having their plates and cups helped the new camp feel more like home.

Each family had a corner where they could set up their things. Bunk beds made of boards nailed together with room for every member made everyone happy. Indeed, this was luxury.

Mamma was grateful for what she had. Her children were healthier than they had been. She still didn't know if Pappa was alive or dead. If he was alive, she didn't know if he was free or in prison. If he was a prisoner, was he being tortured? Yet she had her children—all of them—and that was something not many other mothers in the refugee camps could claim.

During the day, the children played outside. There were many children, but some of them were thin and sickly. They needed nutrition that wasn't available. Diseases also ravaged this camp; children were covered with sores. Many suffered from runny noses and coughs. Diphtheria was rampant. Children became ill from typhus, typhoid fever, and dysentery. Some children developed tuberculosis. One of the male refugees had become crippled during the war and was left to care for his two small children when his wife died of diphtheria. Because of his physical limitations, other refugees helped him care for his children.

In these refugee camps, some things remained the same. Fleas and lice were busy here as well. The Reimer children had their own personal weapon to kill the bedbugs: a broken knife they brought from home. This *wanzen messer* [bedbug knife] was put down in the slats of the bed to kill the bugs. It became a game to see which child could kill the most bugs in an evening. Mamma did her best to keep her children clean, but the fleas and lice were a never-ending concern. Camp Hasselö had a barrack that was called the Isolation Barrack. The window panes were painted white so no one could see inside. No one ever announced when someone was taken to the Isolation Barrack, but everyone learned quickly that when a person went into this barrack, he did not come out alive.

One family the Reimer children enjoyed playing with was the Rüpert children. Gabriella was Ruth's age, and they spent a lot of time together. Herbert and Hannelore were younger, and sometimes Hannelore was not happy when the older girls went off to play by themselves, excluding her. Nevertheless, Gabrielle and Ruth knew there were so many other children of all ages and sizes who needed playmates, and Hannelore found playmates in those children. The girls learned to know each other well since both families were housed in the same barrack. Each family had its own corner in the barrack.

Elveera, another of Ruth's friends, and her mother were in another corner of the barrack. The fourth corner was claimed by a mother with three adult daughters. The woman and her adult daughters looked out for others, especially those in their barrack. As it became colder outside, the refugees were concerned about the winter since heating their own barrack was the responsibility of the refugees. A stove in the middle of the barrack was used to provide heat in winter months. Anything that could be burned to provide heat was used, and for the refugees, a constant concern was keeping supplies on hand for heating. This led to pilfering and stealing.

These women scoured the camp, looking for items that could be burned. Mamma stood guard while the women found wood items to confiscate. They didn't give her any choice; somebody had to stand guard, and they were the ones taking the risk of stealing. Even so, Mamma was afraid they would be caught, and it bothered her that they stole things for later burning. Yet what could she do? They needed to stay warm, and if these women didn't take things, someone else would get them. Sometimes they burned boards from their beds. Even though the daughters knew the guards would be inspecting their barrack, they took slats and pieces from their beds. The guards either never noticed or chose to ignore the missing wood pieces when they made inspections. These treasured sources for winter heat were kept in the ceiling of the barrack. In addition to boards and straw ticks, they found old wagons or pieces of carriages that they hoarded for later kindling. Mamma was grateful for the help of this woman and her three daughters. Their barrack was much warmer during the cold winter because of their diligence in finding burning materials for their stove.

Mamma enjoyed finding other relatives in the camp, as well as other Mennonite folk with last names such as Bench and Schwartz. Some of these relatives did not know each other well before the war. Nevertheless, blood was thicker than water, and family was family, no matter how distantly they were related or how little they knew each other before the war.

Camp life continued day in and day out. Danish guards with guns on their backs guarded the camps so no one could escape. No one was allowed out of the camp, and no one was allowed in without permission. Yet sometimes during the night, refugees managed to leave anyhow. One of the adult girls slipped out across the fence in the night several times to visit the town. She learned to know a young man in town, and he became her boyfriend. This girl continued to sneak out at night. Did the guards never notice, or did they see and turn their heads?! Their secret meetings continued for a while, and sometimes the boyfriend came into the camp at night to spend time with this girl. Once he brought a camera with him and offered to take a picture. This was the only photo taken of the children during their years in refugee camps. This photo shows dresses shorter than they usually wore because they had outgrown almost all their clothing. (Mamma used skirts that the girls outgrew to make clothing for little Dieter.)

It was exciting to know about the nighttime escapades, but it was also scary. What if they were caught? Did the guards know and not care, or were they just waiting for the right time to arrest this girl?! Did they somehow know this girl would not cause any trouble? Did they feel sorry for the girl and think she should be allowed to experience some normalcy in her life? Could Ruth and

Refugee Camp at Hasselö with Mamma holding Heidi, Lisa, Hans, Ruth, and Dieter.

her siblings get in trouble even though they were not part of the escapades?

While the conditions of the camp were a concern for the adults, the children left their cares behind them and spent a lot of time playing outside. Lack of equipment simply led to creativity and use of their imaginations. They were never bored. With so many children, there were plenty of ideas for things to do, games to play, and many ingenious ways to improvise. The sound of children at play was a constant daytime sound.

"Let's play ball!" Hannie called. The children came running to hit their fabric-covered newspaper ball with a wooden stick. It exploded, and newspaper fragments of a once sturdy ball drifted to the ground.

"Go find some more newspaper!," Herbert Rüpert called.

"We can't play ball without a ball!"

"Guess not," Hannie said.

"Hey!," his face brightened. "Let's play Click!"

"Yeah!," the other children chorused.

In no time, the children were busy—and occupied—with their new game. They forgot their hunger and too-small clothing as they vied for the best position in the game.

[To play this game sometimes called the "stick game," blocks with pointed ends were used. The blocks were more rectangular than round and resembled a long stick. They were six to seven inches in length, with Roman numerals carved on the block. A hole was made in the ground, and the block was put on top of the hole. Holding a longer stick, a child tried to hit the point. When the block flew up, it was hit with the stick while in mid-air, and the length of its flight was measured. The winner was the child whose block had the longest flight. To win at this game took skill and dexterity. There were ways to hit the block and places to hit the block that increased its flight and speed!]

The children also enjoyed playing hopscotch. They constantly scoured the ground to find items they could use for the game. Finding a piece of glass in the dirt on the grounds they could use for this game was cause for delight. When they tired of hop-scotch, they played *Messer Stich,* or "war."

To play *Messer Stich* [knife stick], they took turns throwing a knife into the ground. The winner of this game was the one who "conquered the land." Two squares of "land" were marked out in the dirt. Each child had his own "land," and took turns throwing a knife into his opponent's "land." From the point where the knife landed to the edge of the land border was claimed by the child. The game continued until one opponent was able to claim the entire land belonging to his opponent. Sometimes there was just a small corner left. To have the tip of the knife land directly in that spot took expertise. If the knife did not stand upright in the land a child was trying to conquer, he could claim no territory. If a child's knife fell over on the other person's land, he lost all the land. The person who claimed the entire piece of his opponent's land first was the winner.

Another game that the children enjoyed playing was Battleship. A paper with graph lines was used. The paper was labeled in columns of A, B, C, etc. horizontally. The vertical columns were listed in numerical order of 1, 2, 3, etc. Each participant had the name, number of ship sizes, and ships marked on his paper. The opponent guessed places his ships were. The paper was folded into the shape of an airplane and children guessed where, according to the graph of letters and numbers, the "battleship" would land. The child who sunk the most ships is the winner. [Many years later, Ruth wondered why they played games such as "War" and "Battleship" when their plight was the result of the war. Perhaps this shows their innocence.]

Often when the other children were outside playing, Dieter could not be found. He wasn't outside playing with the other children, and he hadn't found his way to another barrack to play with another child. After looking for him, Mamma usually found him lying on his bed in the barrack. Dieter seemed to be tired, and he slept a lot. [Mamma would learn years later that Dieter probably had TB, but his body was able to heal on its own.]

One day Ruth found Lisa in the barrack cutting pieces from the straw tick. Then she used green and blue woolen threads to embroider designs into the pieces of the straw tick. There were pieces of white paper there as well.

"What are you doing?" Ruth asked Lisa.

"I'm making an autograph album," Lisa replied. "I might as well have something to do, and I can have my friends sign my book. It will help me to remember my friends once we go back home."

"That is a good idea," Ruth encouraged her. "You will make it look good, I know."

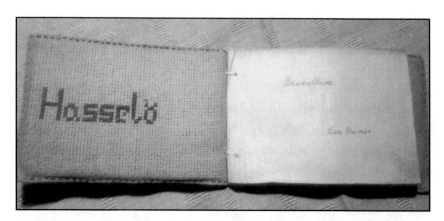

"I'm going to use the blue wool to put a boat on the back cover," Lisa said. "It will remind me of the boat ride we took to get to Denmark."

"I don't know that I even want to remember that boat ride," Ruth replied.

"Well, I do," Lisa responded. "It was horrible, but we made it to Denmark, thanks to Captain Schlickman."

"Yes, we did," Ruth replied. "So much has happened. I miss Pappa. Do you think he is okay?"

Lisa continued embroidering the straw tick pieces as she worked on the cover for her book. "I am sure he is okay, Ruth," she replied. "At least I hope so!"

"Maybe one day we will all be together," Ruth responded. "I hope that is soon! I am tired of being hungry."

"We're all tired of being hungry, Ruth," Lisa replied.

Everyone was hungry! Refugees foraged in the camp, looking for extra food. Some evenings, Mamma didn't eat her rations and let the children have her food. It wasn't much anyway. Hannie was good at picking up pea shells, cabbage leaves, or other peelings that were thrown outside the kitchen window. He brought the food morsels to his family and shared the pea shells and cabbage leaves or anything else he could find.

At mealtimes, boys from the camps were sent to the barracks to call people for supper. One barrack at a time was called, as everyone brought their personal tin cans with handles. With the other refugees, they formed long lines at the window to the kitchen. After one barrack was through the line, another barrack was called.

"Never have to wonder what we're going to have," Hannie grumbled one day. "Soup. Soup with pea peelings. Soup with cabbage peelings. Soup with carrot peelings. Always soup. Nothin' but soup. Sometimes cream of wheat soup!"

"It doesn't matter if you are in the front of the line or the back, it's always the same," Lisa said. "No matter when you get your food, it's always soup. No seconds to be had. Just soup. I wonder if we will ever not be hungry again?" she mused.

"Well, if we ever get out of here and go home, I am not going to be complaining about being hungry anymore. I thought I knew what it felt like to be hungry, but I didn't," Hannie kicked the dust with his feet.

"Everyone here is hungry," Ruth reminded him. "You are not the only one."

"Remember the good food we had at home in Prussia?" Hannie reminisced, rubbing his stomach.

"Of course, I remember!" Lisa said. "We had bread with honey for breakfast. Sometimes we had cheese and meat."

"And coffee," Mamma said wistfully.

"At lunchtime we had potatoes and vegetables and meat," Hannie reminded them.

"I remember the milk soup we had for supper, and potatoes, and bread," Lisa added.

"I miss Mamma's pancakes," Ruth interjected, "with fried eggs and mashed potatoes."

"And on Sundays, we had salt potatoes," Hannie remembered. "Now it feels like we are in a prison!"

"We don't have any place else to go. We are at the mercy of the people of Denmark. Who knows where Pappa is or if we will ever see him again?," Lisa replied.

"I wish we could be with Pappa," Hannie said wistfully. "Do you think he is okay? Is he trying to find us?"

"He will find us. Pappa will look for us until he finds us," Lisa assured her brother.

"But what if he doesn't know we are in Denmark? What if he just looks in Germany?"

"Pappa will find us. He has to find us," Lisa replied tearfully.

"Cheer up, children. We will find Pappa or he will find us," Mamma said firmly.

"We must try to stay clean and healthy because they won't let us leave if we are sick. Germany won't allow us back in our country if we are too sick. God has taken care of us and He will keep on taking care of us!"

"I just want to go back to our country," Lisa said.

"We all want to go back, Lisa," Mamma said. "Let's be grateful for what we have."

Mamma paused a little, then she smiled and said, "I have something else to tell you."

The children's faces waited expectantly.

"You will be starting school soon."

"School? There's no school here," Hannie scoffed.

"You don't need a building to have school. The children are going to be divided into groups by ages. We will tell stories and sing songs, and children who don't know how to read will be taught how to read," she explained. "We will use the large dining room for our school. That dining room is empty since we never use it for eating," she said.

"Younger children will be taught the alphabet and their numbers. And they will practice writing," Mamma's voice was excited.

"How can they teach them to write when there is no paper and no pencils?," Lisa asked.

"They will think of something, I am sure," Mamma answered. "It is important that you keep learning. There are so many people here with many talents, and there are many teachers among the refugees! Some of them will teach children the alphabet. Other people will find a way to do art projects. Everybody is going to work together so you children can have school. When we get to go back home, you need to be prepared to return to school. You don't need books or papers to learn. There are always the catalogs we use for toilet paper. We can use some of those until we find a way to get more."

School started as promised. The children were gathered into the dining room and divided into groups by ages. Women who had been schoolteachers took on the task of teaching children to read and write. Others were assigned to tell stories. Some taught the children songs and how to sing. At first, there were no crayons, pencils, books, or writing paper. The children used toilet paper for writing until writing paper became available. In time, word spread to relief organizations that refugee children were going to school without any supplies.

A few weeks later, paper and pencils arrived in the camps. Relief organizations, including MCC, had heard about the plight of the children and sent supplies. Now there was paper for studying arithmetic and practicing penmanship. The pencils were cut into several pieces so each child could have one.

One day, a care package arrived for Mrs. Reimer. This package had been shipped from America, and it held many wonderful items! Inside the package was soap, coffee, chocolate, thread, and notebooks. The package came through MCC.

"Who sent the package, Mamma?" the children asked, crowding around her as she pulled each item from the box. "We don't know anybody in America."

"Some wonderful people in America put packages together. Many Mennonite people are trying to help us after the war. Oh, how good God is to provide for us in this way!"

Spring turned into summer. In the camp, refugees learned that mail could once again be delivered from Germany to Denmark. What excitement as the refugees waited to hear from family members back home or in other refugee camps!

Mamma and her children prayed daily for Pappa. They prayed that he was safe and that he would be able to find them or that they would be able, somehow, to find him.

Newspapers provided entertainment. Children saved photos of people and pictures. Some newspapers had a little bear and little girl in the right-hand corner. Children cut out the bear and the girl and collected them. According to the newspaper, the bear's name was Bamse and the girl's name was Liesel. It was fun trading Liesel and Bamse with other children.

One day Lisa found scraps of raincoats and other torn up pieces of plastic. This gave her an idea.

"I'm going to make some things with this," she instructed Ruth. "I'll make some toys and trinkets with this plastic. If you find any more pieces, save them for me."

"Okay, I will. But what are you going to do with them?" Ruth asked her sister.

"We can play with the animals and sit the trinkets around to help make our barrack look nicer," Lisa explained.

"I don't know how you do that," Ruth told Lisa. "You are creative, and I am not. But these will be nice to have and take with us when we go home."

Perhaps Lisa had learned to be resourceful from watching her mamma and others in the camp. Each adult received one stamp a month. Adults traded postage stamps with each other. Everyone learned to barter and to think ahead to what was the most important for

them. Some adults wanted coffee. Others wanted postage stamps to exchange for food or other items.

Throughout the camp, refugees learned to share with each other. In celebration of one of the children's birthdays, Mamma saved several pieces of bread and bartered for some pudding. She got permission to toast the bread in the camp kitchen and then put the toasted bread together with the pudding to make a birthday cake for her child. Even though the family was displaced, birthdays were cause for celebration!

One very special day in April 1946, a letter came to the camp addressed to Mamma. It was from Pappa! Mamma was the first person in her barrack to receive a letter.

"Children," Mamma's hands shook as she opened the letter. "Look! A letter from Pappa! I can hardly believe my eyes! How did he know where to find us?! Look!!," she said, pointing to the postmarks on the envelope. "He sent it to Camp Gedser and they forwarded it to me here!"

"What does it say?" the children crowded around her, waiting.

"Let's see." Mamma unfolded the paper, her hands still trembling. "He is working on a farm in northern Germany and is trying very hard to have us come to the farm with him. Pappa is waiting for us to come. Isn't this wonderful news?!" Mamma's face shone.

Finally, they knew. They knew that Pappa was alive! He was able to work. He wasn't a prisoner (at least not now) and he wasn't injured. Mamma continued reading the letter.

I contacted Mennonite Central Committee. They have a list of names of all the Mennonite people in the refugee camps. I inquired about you and learned from Dr. Ernst Crous that there is a Mrs. Reimer and five children in this camp. That means that there is another baby? Is it a boy or a girl? I am living in northern Germany and am not far from the Danish border. I have a job working for a farmer. He has been good to me. The farmers have been forced to take in refugees, and some of them are angry and bitter. This man is good to work for, and I am grateful.[24]

"There is so much he does not know," Mamma said, clutching the letter. "I must write to him and let him know that we are all okay. I must tell him about little Heidi. He doesn't even know about our baby! Oh, this is such wonderful news! And to think the soldiers told us that all German officers were either dead or in prison camps!"

Mamma found paper and pencil to write to Pappa. She traded coffee for some stamps from another family. Mamma didn't need the coffee as desperately as she needed stamps to write to Pappa.

When Mamma wrote her letter to Pappa, she explained how they had left Prussia for Denmark. In her letter, she told Pappa about Heidi's stay in the hospital, and she included something she had never told her children.

> We have so much to be thankful for. Our children are all well. Yes, there is another baby. I named her Heidelore Liesbet,[25] and she was born on August 13. Heidi was very sick, and they put her in the hospital. One day when I went to visit her, the doctor told me he did not think she would live. When I came back the next week, Heidi was much better. A nurse told me that after I left, they put Heidi in the hallway on a stretcher because they thought she was dead. The nurse walked past the stretcher and saw Heidi move. This Danish nurse picked up our little Heidi and took her home to her house. She nursed her back to health. When she was better, the nurse brought Heidi back to the hospital. We owe God and this nurse the life of our little Heidi. I can hardly wait for you to meet Heidi and see all the other children. They are growing despite the lack of food we have at the camp.

---

[24] Gingerich, p. 26.
[25] Heidilore Liesbet's middle name was after Mamma's relative Liesbet who went with her to the clinic to deliver her baby.

Now the family knew that Pappa was safe. They didn't know when they would see him again, but so many questions had been answered. Not only had their questions been answered; God had answered their prayers.

~ *Chapter Eight* ~

A PLACE IN CAMP OKXBØL

June 1947 - March 1948

Another day an announcement was made. "*Achtung!* [Attention!] *Morgen*, [Tomorrow] all refugees will be moved to another camp," the voice over the loudspeaker said.

There was a lot of chatter among the refugees about this move. Some parents were excited because of what this move might mean.

"I heard that they are moving people together so they can close some of the camps. That must mean that some people have been able to leave and return to Germany," one of the women said.

That evening, the children helped Mamma pack the few things they had. Among the first items were clothing and the smaller blankets Mamma had cut from the larger blanket. Carefully, Ruth and Lisa packed their plates and cups to go with them to their next camp. There were not many other clothes to pack. Most of their clothing was worn out, but they didn't care as long as they had something to wear.

After breakfast the next morning, Mamma and the children boarded the train for the trip to the new camp. It was another crowded train ride. This camp was large, and it was called Camp Okxbøl.[26] Hundreds, no, thousands of refugees got off the train and were herded into the camp where there were many barracks. Each barrack was labeled by letter. Mamma entered the barrack to which they were

---

[26] Established in 1945, Camp Okxbøl was located near the Danish North Sea coast. It housed up to 37,000 refugees with 1,247 young children buried in the camp's cemetery.

assigned. It was labeled P-2, and the room for her family was number ten.

"You children need to remember where to find our barrack," Mamma instructed them. "This camp is so much larger than Camp Gedser. I heard it has room for over 35,000 refugees. Always remember to find the section for the P barracks. We are in building 2 of the P barrack section."

"Yes," Hannie interjected. "I heard that the Q barracks are for people who are *Verrütkt* [crazy]. You don't want to get lost over there."

"How much longer do you think we will need to stay in camps, Mamma?" Lisa asked. "I would just like to go back home."

"I don't know, Lisa," Mamma answered. "We have to have a place to live when we go back to Germany. If we hear from Pappa, we will have a better idea." Mamma's face was sober again.

Then she smiled. "Come, children! Let's start by getting unpacked."

Even as she spoke, Mamma was looking around the room. It was dirty, but her children knew she would get it clean. Ruth knew Mamma would make sure they were as clean as they could be.

It didn't take long to unpack their meager belongings. Lisa and Ruth unpacked their plates and cups they had brought from home, and Mamma unpacked the blankets for Heidi. Before long, everything was in place.

Mamma sent Lisa and Ruth to the washhouse to get some water. This washhouse had a long trough with plenty of spigots for getting water. There wouldn't be as much of a wait in line for water at this camp, Ruth realized.

On the way back with the water, Ruth said, "Remember how the servants carried water from Lake Lashken in buckets with a yoke across their shoulders? That seems like such a long time ago."

"Yes," Lisa answered. "It makes me miss home. I loved going to the Lashken and playing there. The flowers were so pretty. I miss pretty flowers!"

"Me, too," Ruth was wistful. "I miss the Lashken, too. There are no lakes like that here!"

"I wonder how much longer it will be until we can go home." Lisa was wistful. "You would think that since the war is over, we could go back to our country."

"I wonder what our farm looks like," Ruth wondered aloud. "Do you think the Russians found our furs and rifles? Did they find Mamma's china?"

"I wonder how Oma is doing. Do you think she is okay? I miss our Omas." Lisa was somber.

Ruth nodded. There were so many questions, and not many answers.

So much had happened since Staschow took them to the port near Danzig. Ruth's clothing was thinner and practically worn out; and it had become much too small for her. Her shoes were worn out. Denmark and Holland sent clothing and wooden shoes. Countries who had been resisting the Nazis responded to Germany's refugees by providing shelter and clothing, but the Reimer children were too young to realize the significance of Germany's former enemies helping them.

"It's hard to walk in these shoes," Ruth told Mamma.

"Don't fuss, Ruth, dear," Mamma reprimanded. "Be glad you have something to wear on your feet. Be glad you have feet that can walk. Be glad that we are all here together."

Be glad, be glad, be glad, Mamma said, but Mamma didn't look that happy. The lines on her face seemed deeper and wider now. Her body was thinner. Mamma's face had a pinched look, and sometimes Ruth saw Mamma sitting on her bed, just staring into the corner.

Ruth rubbed her stomach. It was always empty. If only they could have more food than just soup and a piece of bread. But they were civilian prisoners of war, and Denmark was doing the best it could to help the many German refugees who had invaded their country.

"Children, we are allowed to go for a walk outside the camp today, but a guard will go with us," Mamma told them. "You must always walk straight. Don't shuffle around. Walk like you are proud. The Danish soldiers will carry guns, but they won't hurt you if you walk straight; don't go left or right." For the children it was fun to go outside and see something new.

"Walk straight and walk tall," Mamma told them over and over.

They walked straight and tall, but it was still fun to get out of the camp. Even though they were still prisoners, it was nice to be able to go someplace else and see other people. The walk was invigorating. The soldiers didn't mind if children didn't stay in a straight line. They didn't seem worried that anyone would try to escape. Where would they go if they did run away? There was no place else to go, and the soldiers knew this. They knew children would want to go back to their mothers who stayed behind in the camp. They knew adults would not leave elderly parents or small children. The walk was leisurely and fun.

Mamma went along on one of the walks, but she didn't enjoy herself. She felt demeaned walking with the guardsmen carrying guns over their shoulders. "You can go with the others," she told the children, "but be sure to walk straight. Don't go left or right."

By this time, Ruth had seen many soldiers of many different ranks. She was used to having soldiers at the camps. The soldiers didn't smile much, but that was okay. She knew they would not hurt her. Ruth also remembered conversations about the German army when they had lived in Germany.

"We are going to overrun the Danish!" the German soldiers who lived at her house had said emphatically. Somehow, the German soldiers had not been able to overrun the Danish. Even though the German soldiers were enemies of the Danish people, the Danes were feeding the German refugees. Even though Germany had been at war against the Allies, the Danish country had allowed the refugees inside their borders.

The children found new as well as old playmates in this camp that housed 38,000 German refugees. There were plenty of ideas for play and how to play. While the children enjoyed being outdoors, the adults liked being inside, away from the guards and all the other refugees. There was solace in staying "home" even though it wasn't home.

One of the games the children improvised was a counting game. First, a child threw a ball against a wall ten times, hitting it with his fist when the ball came back. Then he had to use his arm nine times to hit the ball, never allowing it to hit the ground. Next, he hit it eight times with his head, and so on. If the ball hit the ground, the player was out, and another child had a turn. In their play, they learned cooperation and fun. They also learned math even though they were unaware they were developing such skills.

In addition to learning subjects and skills, Mamma kept teaching poems and songs to her children. She encouraged them to pray every night.

The prayer Ruth prayed every night was simple, but she never forgot this prayer:

Ich bin klein, mein Herz ist rein.
Soll niemand drin wohnen als Jesus allein.
[I am little. My heart is clean.
Nobody should live in it (my heart) but Jesus alone.]

As the seasons changed, the refugees attempted to prepare for colder weather. This was hard to do, for they had little with which to barter. As it became colder and colder outside, the children shivered in their thin coats. There were no decorations to put up to celebrate Christmas except for the small Christmas tree in the hall of the barrack.

On Christmas Eve, women and children gathered together. Christmas, a time that used to be so happy and joyful, was just another day this year. They huddled in groups, and some evenings they sang familiar Christmas songs. There were no gifts.

"It's Christmas," Mamma said, "and we have no gifts. But we have each other and we are all together, but Pappa. This Christmas, we know that Pappa is okay."

And we are all cold, and dirty, and hungry, Ruth thought. She didn't dare say those words out loud. It would make Mamma feel bad. There was nothing Mamma could do, but what she was doing: keeping them as clean and as warm as she could.

Here in Denmark, it was cold just like in West Prussia. Ruth missed Christmas with her family in their house. In Prussia, Christmas was a happy time. The family's big celebration was on Christmas Eve. Mamma and the maids spent a lot of time baking. Lisa's and Ruth's dolls often disappeared before Christmas; and when they opened their gifts, they found their dolls with new clothing that Mamma had made for them. The workers were invited to come join the celebration.

On Christmas Eve, everyone gathered around the Christmas tree. Candles on the tree were lit, and Pappa would read the Christmas story. Singing was always fun, and each year they sang Christmas songs. One of Ruth's favorites was *Stille Nacht* [Silent Night]. It was the only time of the year that the Bible was taken off the shelf and read out loud. Before the children could open their gifts, they had to recite a new Christmas poem they had learned. Some years, Pappa had made dollhouses and barns. Occasionally, he made new sleds for his children who loved to go sled riding in the winter. In addition to toys and gifts, the children and workers received a dish with cookies, candies, and fruits. The children got homemade gifts such as knit socks or knit sweaters. On Christmas Day, the candles on the Christmas tree were lit again. It seemed like such a long time since those Christmas days. Would they ever have Christmas like that again? What fun it would be to have a new sled or dolls to play with this Christmas! It wasn't going to happen, Ruth knew.

Ruth remembered one poem she memorized and recited before she could open her gifts one year.

Weihnachtsstadt
A Christmas Poem
von Theodor Storm

Vom Himmel in die tiefsten Klüfte
Ein milder Stern herniederlacht;
Vom Tannenwalde steigen Düfte
und hauchen durch die Winterlüfte,
Und kerzenhelle wird die Nacht

Mir ist das Herz so froh erschrocken.
Das ist die liebe Weihnachtszeit!
Ich höre fernher Kirchenglocken
Mich lieblich heimatlich verlocken
In märchenstille Herrlichkeit.

Ein frommer Zauber hält mich wieder,
Anbetend, staunend muß ich stehn;
Es sinkt auf meine Augenlider
Ein goldner Kindertraum hernieder,
Ich fühl's, ein Wunder ist geschehn.

From Heaven into the deepest chasm
A mild star shines pleasantly down
From the green forests came aromas
And float through the winter air
And the night becomes candlelight bright.

My heart is filled with awe
That is the dear Christmastime
From far away I hear Christmas bells
To entice me to homesickness
In fairytale quiet beauty.

An innocent magic keeps me calm
Worshiping amazed I am standing here
A golden dream of my childhood comes over me
I feel a miracle happened.

This Christmas, officers in the camp promised that Santa Claus would come and bring gifts. The children sat up that night, waiting expectantly. Surely Santa will come! Ruth thought. Lisa, Hannie and Ruth stayed up late that night.

Sometimes the wind blew a branch across the roof top.

"Maybe that's him!" Hannie whispered.

Then the silence came again, and Hannie realized it had just been the wind.

For hours, they sat up, waiting. *Maybe Santa will bring some fruit—or even some candy,* Ruth thought. *Maybe he'll bring me some new clothes, or some shoes that don't hurt my feet . . . maybe he'll bring me a doll like Alice . . . .*

Maybe never happened. Santa never came.

In the morning, Hannie was woebegone. "Mamma," he said quietly, "Santa missed our barracks."

Mamma smiled at Hannie. "Do you know what I thought about last evening, Hannie?" she asked.

"What?" he asked.

"I thought about another Christmas Eve. Your Pappa came to my home, and we celebrated our engagement with our parents and friends. We had such a fun time celebrating! That was 15 years ago. I wonder where he is now," she said quietly.

Then her face brightened. "Come, children, we will celebrate Christmas together! We have each other, and everybody is healthy."

That Christmas morning, the children still had to recite the verses Mamma had made them learn. When Mamma packed for the trip out of the country, she had put a book of verses in her satchel. Each child had to learn his own verse. There were no presents, but they still had each other, and they knew Pappa was well.

Engagement photo of Johannes and Gerda Reimer.

One of the older refugee ladies in the camp was Kathe Federau,[27] a well-known poet. She wrote poems for Christmas. This year, the poem she wrote was this one:

> *Der stern von Bethlehem scheint über alle Trümmer*
> *Und relbst der Flüchtling spürt dan warmen Schein*
> *So machet Platz dem gold'nen*
> *Weihnachtschimmer*
> *Das liebe Christkind legt ihn selbest hinein.*

> [The star of Bethlehem shines over all the ruins
> And even the refugee feels its warm glow
> So make room for the golden Christmas shimmer
> The dear Christ child will put it in Himself.]

A powerful influence in the lives of children in the camp was Peter Dyck. Peter and his wife Elfreida worked for MCC, visiting

---

[27] The copy of this poem is from Ruth's memory. To her knowledge, it was never published.

refugee camps in Europe. Dyck told Bible stories and taught songs to the children. It was evident to adults and children alike that their plight resonated with him. A Russia-born lad, he and his family had experienced help from Mennonites in Canada during the Revolution at the start of the Soviet Union. Now he was giving back to others and sharing the good news of the gospel in his travels across war-torn Europe. The Bible stories and songs taught by Peter stayed with the children even after his departure to visit another camp. Dyck also passed out small picture cards for the children. The delightful colors in the pictures added warmth and hope to the bleakness of life in the refugee camp.

Ruth and her family looked forward to letters from Pappa. He told them about the farmer he was working for and the many tasks that he was able to do to earn money. In one letter, he wrote about something special that happened:

> *In January, I received a package from a family in America. Their name is Bontrager. I am very fortunate to have been provided clothes in my forced need. I was especially pleased with the underclothing because I have very few pieces of garments and underclothing. I only had one tattered suit when I arrived here, but these good people helped me in my need.*[28]

In the dismal bleakness of the camp, Mamma recognized that they had not been forsaken. Hearing from Pappa about the new clothing he had received made her realize how destitute he was—and how graciously God had provided.

A few months later, a note came from the Camp leader. It said, "In ten to fourteen days, a package from America will be delivered to you."

---

[28] Letter from Johannes Reimer, to the Bontrager family, Feb. 22, 1947.

"I can hardly wait!" Hannie said. "I wonder what will be in the package this time!"

"Maybe some more food," Lisa said.

"Or some clothes," Ruth added, remembering the previous package.

Every night until the package came, Ruth went to bed, whispering to herself, *In ten to fourteen days, in ten to fourteen days . . . How many days will it be? Is the package now on a big boat coming across the ocean? What is in the package?* Ruth was so excited! Tonight, she smiled as she drifted off to sleep, thinking, *In ten to fourteen days . . . in ten fourteen days . . . .*

When the package finally arrived, there was such excitement! The children gathered around the package and watched Mamma open it carefully. Soap, coffee, washcloths, and towels! Soft, plush items that were new and not worn out! Soap to help stay clean, and even coffee.

Mamma's greatest concern was the health and safety of her children. She was especially concerned about her younger children, since they were more susceptible to disease. Many of the children in these camps, especially those under the age of three, did not survive. Poor nutrition and disease robbed parents of their children day after day. This is why Mamma guarded her children carefully. She took extra care to keep them healthy. Even though their clothes were becoming ragged and worn, she did her best to keep their clothing clean. There was no reason to argue with Mamma, because she was firm. It didn't matter if there was not enough soap. There was water, and they would be as clean as possible.

One day Ruth found Mamma inside the barrack, pulling the wool thread from a full slip she had brought with her.

"Mamma, why are you taking your slip apart?," Ruth asked.

"I'm going to use it to make something for baby Heidi," Mamma explained. "She needs clothes to wear and she needs this more than I need the slip." Mamma's hands were quick as she pulled the wool yarn from the slip and knitted it into a garment for baby Heidi.

Ruth marveled at what her mother could do. She made new things out of old ones. When clothing became too small, she took it apart and made something else. Sometimes she made shorts for Dieter out of clothing that Ruth had outgrown. Mamma had thought ahead when she packed and had brought a small pillowcase with yarn, needles, and scissors from home. Now that yarn and those needles was helping to keep her children dressed. She was a good seamstress, but she didn't need a sewing machine to fix and make things. She could do so much with her knitting needles, sewing needle, and thread!

"I am so grateful that my parents sent me to school for cooking, preserving, and sewing. I never dreamed I would be able to use what I learned here, but it certainly has helped me keep my family clothed," she said, stitching quickly and evenly.

In Camp Okxbøl, there were unfinished barracks where Danish workers came each day to work and prepare housing for more refugees. Sometimes the workers sat outside the barracks on benches to eat the lunch they had brought from home.

Ruth had not seen such delicious food for so long, it seemed! Sandwiches with meat and cheese and real German bread instead of sourdough bread! Apples and fruit! It was hard for the hungry children to see that delicious food and know it was not theirs to take. Some days, some of the workers shared some of their lunch with the children.

"Mamma!" Hannie exclaimed as he found Mamma in their barrack one day, "Some of the men working in the barracks gave us some of their lunch! I had an apple. A real apple. It was sooo good!"

"Children, you must not ask these men for food; you must not beg."

"We didn't beg," Hannie assured her. "They asked us if we wanted some, and of course, I said yes. He gave it to me. He watched me eat it, and he smiled."

After that, the children often hung around the workers, hoping for more offers of food. They were not often disappointed. While still hungry even after eating these delicious morsels, for the moment, the satisfaction of food other than broth and a piece of hard bread was a delight.

Hannie watched hopefully for trucks coming into the camp. He knew the trucks carried food such as turnips. Whenever possible, the children tried to take a few turnips from the truck. Sometimes they could pick them from the ground where they'd fallen off the truck. Other times they pilfered from the load on the truck. The children knew which guards and which drivers would take pity on those daring thieves and ignore them. Sometimes, the guards threw some turnips off the truck so the children could pick them up.

Hannie generously took the turnips to Mamma to share with the family.

"Hans! You must not do this!" Mamma scolded. "You know that we can be sent away from the camp if you are caught."

"I know, Mamma," Hannie said, "but I know which guards will look the other way and I only take a few. I take them when I know the guards won't do anything. I am being careful, I promise. And sometimes, Mamma, they even let some turnips roll off the truck. I am sure they are throwing some down for us to get. We are all so hungry . . . " his voice drifted off as he rubbed his stomach.

Hans was getting taller, and his clothes were shorter and tighter on him. Hans was hungry. He was now eleven, and now his family sometimes called him Hans instead of Hannie. Was it because he was getting older, or partly because he had become the man of the family, looking after his mother and siblings, giving unselfishly to help them all survive?

Even so, his body needed nutrition for his growing years. He needed more than soup and a piece of bread. Each turnip and each apple added more sustenance to his frame.

A few days later another announcement was made over the loudspeakers in the camp.

"*Bekannt Machung!* [Announcement!] This camp will be closing, so all refugees will be moving to another location."

Once again, Mamma and the children packed their few belongings. Mamma still had the baby carriage and Lisa and Ruth each had a cup and plate they had brought from home. It didn't take long to pack up their meager belongings and be ready for the move to the next camp.

~ Chapter Nine ~

A PLACE IN CAMP SKRÜDSTRUP

April 1948 - October 1948

"This camp will get us ready to go back home," Mamma explained to her family after they were settled into their new barrack. Then she smiled wryly.

"Not that we really have a home, but we have a place where we can live. We will have to show them that we have a place to stay and someone to help take care of us. Pappa is writing letters to tell them that he will have a place for us to live and that he has a job and can take care of us."

There was a strict rule in Camp Skrüdstrup that anyone caught stealing would be prohibited from being released. Doing anything unlawful (such as lying about where he would go to live) was not permitted, either.

"Children," Mamma told them one day, "This is a strict rule. You must not steal anything from anybody. I know you are hungry, but if you steal and the guards find out, we will not be allowed to be released. We will be required to stay here. Don't you want to go see Pappa again?" she begged.

They nodded enthusiastically. Of course, they wanted to see Pappa, but they were also hungry, and it was hard to say no to the temptation when food was available to take.

Camp Skrüdstrup was surrounded on both sides by orchards. The farmers on each side of the enclosed fence had an abundance of fruit. On the one side was a farmer who had apples and pears. His workers made large piles of picked apples and pears near the fence. If a friendly guard was on duty or if an unfriendly guard wasn't watching, the workers were permitted to toss some of the fruit over the fence.

Children scrambled for the fruit, sharing it among themselves. Hans grabbed as many apples as he could hold and ran to their barrack. As Hans ran across the threshold, the apples he had hidden under his shirt slid out onto the floor. He stooped down to pick them up as they rolled across the floor.

"Hans!" Mamma said. "What is this?!"

"It's apples, Mamma, apples! Now we have something good to eat!"

"Hans! Where did you get these apples?" Mamma asked, running her fingers over their skins and turning them in her hands. She could almost taste them now.

"I know nobody saw me. I was careful, and nobody was there except other children also getting the apples." Hans clamped his teeth on the apple and took a huge bite. "We are all hungry. Have some, Mamma. It will be good for you," he urged, chomping happily.

The other children clamored around, each reaching for an apple and sinking their teeth into the juicy fruit. Fresh apples! How long had it been since they had been able to enjoy fresh fruit?

Mamma straightened her shoulders. She looked at Hans, and she looked right into his eyes.

"Hans Reimer! Did you steal them? Did you STEAL these apples?"

"No, Mamma, I didn't. The farmer from the farm next to the camp threw them across by the fence. We saw him throw them across and we ran to get them!"

"Oh Hans, you need to be careful! What if the guards think you are stealing them?!"

"We didn't steal them, Mamma. The farmer threw them over the fence. He wanted us to have the apples," Hans defended his actions.

"Listen to me, son. I know you are hungry. We are all hungry. It is wrong to steal, especially when they have made this announcement. We want to go back to Germany and back to Pappa. If you are caught stealing, we won't be able to go back there."

Hans nodded. "I know, Mamma. It wasn't stealing when he put them there for us. Plus, we all watched, and no one saw us."

Mamma shook her head as she took the apple Hans offered to her.

"You must be careful, children. If we want to leave, we must be careful so the guards won't find any reason to keep us here," Mamma said, taking a bite of the apple and savoring its sweet juiciness.

The children nodded. They knew Mamma was concerned, but they also knew the apples were a gift to them from a Danish farmer they did not even know.

On the other side of the camp was another farmer who also had an orchard. Day after day, he came near the fence, picked up several apples, and raised his arm as if he was going to throw some apples over the fence. Children watched, waiting to catch whatever fruit was tossed to them. But instead of releasing the apples from his hands, he dropped his arms and discarded the apples on the ground. One day he dug a hole in the ground and buried the apples. The heinous smile on his face as he covered the apples told the children he was not their friend after all.

"If I ever have a lot of food, I am going to share it with anybody who needs it!" Hans clenched his fists as the children walked dejectedly back to the barracks.

"It's not fair!" Lisa said. "He is just going to throw those apples away. He won't use them, and he could give them to people who are hungry, like us!"

Ruth felt the gnawing in her stomach. It was always empty! Even after she ate her soup at lunchtime, she was still hungry. Hans was getting taller. The sleeves of his shirt were inches shorter than when they first came to this camp. Hans was hungry, too. Everybody was hungry, for that matter.

Is it wrong to take apples thrown over the fence when we are hungry? There were plenty of apples and they were tasty and delightful to eat—how can it be so wrong when we are hungry? Other children are stealing things. I've even seen adults take things. It has happened in every camp. We just want to survive. How can this be so wrong? Ruth pondered.

At first, living in the barracks in the different refugee camps was not so bad. There were other children to play with, and there were no chores. Really, there was no schoolwork to do either. They could play all day. But Ruth missed home. She missed Pappa and the flowers on the farm. She missed the Lashken. She missed playing in the yard with Hans and playing with Mamma's doll Alice with Lisa in the house.

All of that was gone. Those days seemed so far in the past. The same thought kept plaguing Ruth in repetitive waves, as she wondered, *will life ever go back to the way it was? Will Oma be able to keep the farm going until we return? Will we ever see Pappa again? How much longer until we can leave and go back home? Did the war destroy our home? Are the Allied forces in Prussia? Are they occupying our farm and home? Is it still standing or is it crumbling? What does home look like? It is so hard to remember . . . . If Hitler was so right, then why is he dead? Why didn't he want to live to fight? Where is Pappa?*

When Ruth was hungry, it was hard to think clearly. It was hard to feel happy and not be afraid or filled with worry. If there wasn't enough food, would they even survive? The war was over, but for Ruth and her family, it had not really ended. In some ways, the war had only begun.

Not once since they fled Germany had they had real cake, cookies, or candy. There had been no shopping trip to purchase necessities. For over three years, they had been dirty and hungry with no place to call home and no place they belonged. In that time, they learned to take things as they came; to improvise and make something out of nothing.

Other refugees also suffered just as the Reimer family. All the children in the camp were hungry, and dirty, and sickly. Mamma did the best she could!

One day Hans came into the barracks with a piece of bread.

"Hans," Mamma said. "Where did you get that bread? You cannot take food like that."

"I didn't take food, Mamma," Hans assured her. "I got a job sweeping floors for the camp leader. I am also going to carry out ashes. They won't give me money, but they will give me food. Here, come have some!" he invited his family.

The children crowded around the slice of bread. Hans divided the bread evenly among his siblings. Each of them was grateful for just a little bit of bread. It was more than they had on other days. Hans wanted to do something to help—and he found a way by working.

Mamma refused to take any bread. "You go ahead and eat it," Mamma said. "I'm not that hungry. Thank you, Hans. Thank you for trying to help take care of your brother and sisters. I know Pappa would be pleased."

"How long have we been in this camp, Mamma?" Ruth asked. "We have been refugees for three years. My, look how Heidi has grown! From a little baby who was so sick to a little girl who runs around. Just think. She doesn't know any other home but this."

In Camp Skrüdstrup, there was no school. The organization that had worked so well in Camp Okxbøl was not in place here. In addition, the refugees were making plans to leave and return to their families or their homeland. Mamma kept waiting to hear from Pappa that all the paperwork was complete so they could leave, just like other families.

While she was waiting, Mamma continued to focus her time and attention on keeping her children healthy and clean. She recognized that while the things people sent in the care packages from America were given in concern and love, some items were not practical. Colorful, pastel clothing showed dirt and stains quickly. The yellow dress with white trim around the collar, sleeves and hem was impractical to wear during the day. While all the outdoors was a playground with other children, it also harbored a lot of dirt and bugs. Ruth recognized that if she wore this dress for play, Mamma would never be able to get the stains out and it would quickly become dingy and dirty. Nevertheless, one could always find a way to use things, and Ruth decided to wear the yellow dress as a nightgown so it would not become stained in its first day of play.

Chapter Ten

A Place Back in Camp Okxbøl

A Few Weeks in October 1948

Six months later, another announcement over the loudspeaker gave more unwanted news to the refugees in the camp.

"*Durchsagen*! [Announcement!] The British zone of Germany has closed its borders. Therefore, no refugees can go across their border. We will be moving you back to Camp Okxbøl until we can facilitate your move back to Germany."

What a stir this brought to the refugees in the camp. There were questions and much frustration. Why did this happen when they were so close to going home? The refugees talked among themselves to see if anyone knew the reason that no refugees could cross the border. Several had heard discussion about one of the refugees and thought perhaps they had discovered the reason: refugees could not leave the camp unless they verified information that they had a place to go and someone who would provide for them. One of the refugees falsified information. He was being released under the assumption that he had a place to go in Germany. When the border patrol discovered this was not true, the refugee was sent back, and all the borders were closed. One man's lies unfortunately lengthened the stay for thousands of fellow refugees still housed in Denmark.

Because of the lies, the borders were closed. Because the borders were closed, the family had to move back to Camp Okxbøl. Mamma packed their belongings again. The guards did not allow her to keep the army blankets they had been given.

"Those blankets stay right here!" the guard told them as they came with their luggage. "You leave them here. You will need to find other blankets at Camp Okxbøl."

Mamma had no choice but to leave the blankets with the guards. She also hoped that the guards at Camp Okxbøl would give her more blankets when she returned.

Ruth's satchel contained her meager clothing. Tucked inside her yellow nightgown-dress was one plate that made it through every refugee camp without breaking. These treasures from her last Christmas in West Prussia would remain secure and safe, she hoped, until she finally had a place to call home. Lisa made certain she had her autograph album in her belongings. This would stay with her, she knew, for the rest of her life.

Soon they were back at Camp Okxbøl. There were new faces and some old faces from their time there before. Not much had changed in the six months they were gone. The guards at the camp gave Mamma more army blankets for her family. How happy she was to have more blankets for her children, especially since the nights were beginning to grow colder.

Because there were fewer refugee prisoners in the camp, more food was available. Sometimes there was meat, and occasionally real potatoes were served. In addition, the camp was near bodies of water where fish could be easily caught. What a treat it was to be served fish patties!

Sometimes Mamma helped in the kitchen. One Sunday, an especially delicious meal was served for lunch. Meat and potatoes! Although Mamma didn't take any meat, she ate some of the other food.

"There is plenty of meat here," she told her children. "Have some more."

"You don't want any, Mamma?," Ruth noticed she had no meat on her plate.

"I'm just not that hungry," Mamma explained, taking another serving of potatoes. "You go ahead and eat. This is so much better than what we have had in the past."

"I'll take some more," Hans said, heaping more food on his plate. "This is sooo good!"

"Don't talk with your mouth full," Lisa reprimanded.

Mamma smiled at both. "It's been a long time since you've had so much to eat, Hans," she said. "Go ahead and enjoy yourselves, but do mind your manners."

Later, much later, Mamma explained why she hadn't taken any meat. "I helped fix the food the day before, and the meat you had was muskrat. All I could think about was all those muskrats lying on the table with their tails hanging outside the kitchen the day we were fixing it."

Now Pappa's letters came to Camp Okxbøl. Every day Mamma waited, wondering when she and Pappa would be reunited. *Would they be reunited? Would Pappa be able to get the paperwork complete that showed he could provide for his family?*

It was now October 1948. Another announcement was made over the camp loudspeaker.

"The Danish government and the Allied Occupational Forces have reached *Zustimmung* [an agreement] to close our refugee camps and permit German refugees to return to Germany. If you have family members in Germany who can take you in, you will need to provide that information. As soon as the borders are open, you will be able to leave if you can provide the needed information."

This was great news! Pappa had been working diligently to get the papers filled out that said he could provide for his family. His letters told Mamma how hard he had been working, visiting officials to get all the documentation complete so his family could come home.

~ *Chapter Eleven* ~

A PLACE IN CAMP KOLDING

One Night in October 1948

Once again, refugees who had a place to go stood in lines to fill out paperwork. This time, Mamma was one of those refugees! Finally, arrangements were made for Mamma and the children to go to their last camp. This camp was called Kamp Kolding, referred to as *Durhgangslager* [go through]. Kamp Kolding[29] was used to process refugees to return to Germany.

Mamma's face showed her dismay as she surveyed the conditions in this new camp. There was dirt and dust everywhere in their barracks. She didn't say much, but the expression on her face told her children how she felt about staying in this place, even for one night. Yet there was no choice. This was where they were put, and this is where they would spend the night.

"Come, children," she instructed them. "Let's sweep the floors and get settled for the night. Hopefully, we will be able to leave tomorrow."

This camp had no toilets. It housed wooden beds. Mamma tried to help her children get cleaned up as much as they could, because hopefully tomorrow they would see Pappa.

During the night, Ruth heard shuffling and scurrying noises. She lay motionless in bed, listening. *What is it?!!*

She looked at Mamma, who was awake.

"Mamma, I hear something," Ruth whispered.

---

[29] Located in southern Jutland in Denmark. During the war, Germany had a strong presence here, including the Gestapo headquarters for the region.

"Shhh, Ruth, it's just rats. Go back to sleep. They won't hurt you."

In the morning, Mamma seemed tired. This was to be a happy day, because they were going back to Germany to see Pappa.

"I couldn't sleep last night because of the rats," she explained, "but at least we won't need to stay here tonight. Tonight, we will be with Pappa!"

Mamma shook Dieter's shoulder. "Wake up, Dieter," she said. "It's time to get up! Today we are going to ride on the train!"

Mamma bustled about, getting her children up and dressed for this eventful day. She was in a hurry to get her children out of the camp, and not just because she wanted to see Pappa. She wanted to get away from the dirt and those rats.

Could it really be happening? They had waited for so long to go home. It had been three and a half years since they left home. Now they would finally be able to see Pappa.

"Mamma, you are so much thinner than when we last saw Pappa. We all are thinner, even though we are taller," Lisa said.

Mamma looked at Lisa, then she replied, "When I was little and other children were growing taller than me, they would tease me, 'You are getting smaller every day.'[30] Maybe I just got smaller," she smiled.

Refugees lined up, waiting for the guards' inspections and to be given a ticket with their destination. They were all marched to the station to board the train. Ruth carried her satchel with her meager belongings. Inside her satchel was one plate—all that was left from the set she and Lisa had carefully packed when they left home in Danzig almost four years before. There wasn't much else to carry. Most of what they had brought with them was gone. Yet, Mamma left Denmark with what mattered most: every one of her children.

---

[30] Gingerich, p. 7.

Mamma and all her children boarded the train for their last ride to a new home in their homeland. They were leaving Denmark for good.

The war was over, but devastation prevailed in Germany. How had the Danish government managed to provide food and medical care at no charge to the thousands of refugees who came to their land? Would Denmark ever receive compensation for its care of these German civilian prisoners who came uninvited to their shore?

Now it was time to return home to Germany, but Mamma never forgot that her family and her children were safe because of the people in Denmark. Mamma knew that, except for one Danish nurse, Heidi would have been buried in the graveyard at the edge of Camp Gedser in Denmark. Instead, Heidi was healthy and well and would soon be meeting her Pappa for the first time in her three years of life.

"Don't we need tickets?" Hans asked Mamma as they got on board the train.

"No, Hans. The Danish government is putting us on this train. All we need is the ticket that says where we are going."

The children found seats on the wooden benches inside the train. Ruth put her face against the window, waiting for the train to begin moving south. South to her homeland. South to freedom. But would they really, this time, be free?

Ruth was now eleven. *I'm so glad it's dark outside,* Ruth thought. *Pappa won't see how shabby we look, and I'm glad.*

She looked at the bottoms of her old soldier's pants worn under her skirt. They were too short. Her arms protruded from her short sleeves. And those wooden clogs? She would be happy to have other shoes to wear.

But will there be other shoes to wear? Mamma said Pappa would have to work hard to get things we need. But at least we will all be together. That is the most important thing.

Ruth remembered the little girl in the refugee camp who could not hear anymore because of a fever she had that lasted for days.

She remembered the many small children who died in the camps. Hundreds of parents lost their children because of malnutrition and dehydration. Every single one of her family was safe. Tonight, all seven would be together for the very first time. It had been almost four years since they had last seen Pappa. Tonight, he would meet Heidi for the first time!

~ *Chapter Twelve* ~

A PLACE IN DOLLERUP

October 1948 - September 1950

The trip south took several hours and was so different from the one they took north across the Baltic Sea three and a-half years earlier. On that trip, planes were flying overhead, and bombs were exploding in the waters. Tonight, there was just the sound of the train and the odor of smoke from the engine. Passengers sat solemnly, waiting for the train to cross the border into their designated town.

Finally, the train rumbled across the Kaiser Wilhelm Canal. They passed through towns affected by the war. Houses, churches, and factory buildings lay in ruins from the fighting in their homeland. The war had changed the landscape of Germany and had devastated so many hearts.

Refugees on the train sat quietly, looking out the windows. Across the aisles were passengers who obviously were not refugees. They looked poor, too, but not as poor as Ruth and her family. At least those people had some money! Mamma and her children had no money, and as Ruth compared herself to these other travelers, she felt ashamed.

But now, they were coming in to the Flensburg train station. Ruth stared out the window, looking for Pappa. There he was, standing as tall as ever! But he was thin. He looked emaciated. Ruth could see that his face was happy, and that was all that mattered.

One by one, Mamma and the children stepped off the train and flew into Pappa's arms.

"Lisa! How big you have grown!," Pappa exclaimed, hugging her.

"Oh Hans, my boy!" Pappa looked at Hans. Now almost 13, Hans had grown much taller since Pappa had last seen him when he was nine.

And Ruth? Ruth felt Pappa's arms go around her and she hugged him back, conscious of the clothing she was wearing from Denmark: remodeled soldier's coat and trousers, and the black knit stockings with white feet stitched into them. They were poor just like most other Germans, but she was still ashamed. She was happy to see him, but in some ways, he was a stranger to her.

Then Pappa stooped down and took Dieter's hand. "Dieter, my boy," Pappa said. The tears in his eyes grew bigger as he hugged the five-year-old boy.

Pappa reached for Heidi, but she drew back. Who is this strange man?!

Mamma hugged Pappa again and told Heidi, "This is your Pappa. You can hug him. See Mamma hugging Pappa?"

Heidi soon warmed up to this strange man after watching her siblings eagerly and warmly respond to him.

They stood in the train station, together again, a complete family. Back in their homeland. A new home and a new town—but they were together. Tears of happiness filled their eyes. Every one of them had survived the war, and that was what mattered most.

"I borrowed a team of horses and the wagon from the farmer I work for to come and get you," Pappa said, carrying Heidi as he led the way to the wagon.

On the way to their new home, Pappa told Mamma just a little about his time in the prison camp.

"When I realized the war was ending, I knew I would be taken as a prisoner of war. I decided I would rather be a prisoner of the American or British Allies than the Russians, so I made my way over to their side to be captured by one of them. I was captured on May 4, 1945."

"That was while we were on the boat heading to Denmark," Mamma murmured. "How long were you a prisoner?"

"I was a prisoner for over a year. Someday I'll have to tell you how I got released. It is quite the story! I found work here and have been here ever since. We won't have much, but we are together again," he said as he flicked the reins on the horses.

"The money I took with me was collected at the camp; but because of inflation, I could not get any money back after it was exchanged. We were in Denmark too long and the inflation rate was 1:10, so we have nothing left," Mamma told Pappa sadly.

"It does not matter," Pappa assured her quickly. "You took care of our children and now we are all together again."

Pulling the wagon, the horse picked up speed as he was nearing home.

"Das is der hof! [There is the farm!]" Pappa exclaimed. "The farmer I am working for is Herr Lassen."

The lights in the house were on and Pappa guided the horses down the lane right to the door of the house. Herr and Frau Lassen were standing outside, waiting for them.

"Welcome, welcome!" Frau Lassen said.

Pappa made introductions all around.

"We have heard so much about you," Herr Lassen exclaimed, shaking Mamma's hand, "that we feel like we know you already!"

"Come on inside, and we will sit down and eat soon. Let me show you where you can wash up," Frau Lassen said, leading the way to the wash room.

Mamma helped the children wash their faces, arms, and hands so that they would be clean after the train ride and ready for supper. The Lassens had so much! Nice towels and washcloths, and a clean bathroom!

Inside the warm, cozy house, the dining room table was set with a white tablecloth. Fine china and silverware graced the table. In addition, there were real chairs to sit on, one for each of them! Ruth and her family had not eaten with silverware for three and a half years.

"Go sit down with your family, Reimer," Herr Lassen instructed Pappa. He went into the kitchen to help his wife and the maid.

Soon the maid came in carrying a steaming bowl of hot soup. Frau Lassen ladled soup into everyone's bowl.

The house seemed so quiet with only ten people there. Ruth was used to eating surrounded by hundreds of people and a lot of chatter and noise. She was comfortable sitting on a bench or the floor to eat out of tin cans, but everything was so nice here that none of them knew how to act. Everything was strange, and Ruth wasn't even sure she liked eating with a real tablecoth with real plates and silverware. Here there were no guards watching, making sure no one would try to escape or steal something. Here it was just Herr and Frau Lassen and their maid in their farmhouse with Ruth and her family.

Next, the maid brought in a beef stew with boiled potatoes. Fresh, homemade bread and real, homemade butter! Ruth wanted to hold the bread to her nose and inhale the fragrance. How long it had been since she had eaten food like this! At the urging of their hosts, Hans kept adding more food to his plate.

Soon Ruth's stomach was full. The food tasted different; she was so used to bland food that this food didn't even taste right. Her stomach realized it, too. Suddenly, she felt very full. And tired. And sleepy. Little Dieter's and Heidi's eyes were starting to droop.

Frau Lassen stood up. *"Kommen Sie!* [Come!] I know you all are tired. Let me show you where you will sleep tonight. These children need to go to bed."

Ruth and her siblings followed Frau Lassen upstairs to rooms with beds, real beds with real pillows and sheets and covers! No straw ticks, no paper blankets, no army blankets. Just a real bed with a clean feather tick cover!

Is this really true, or am I only dreaming? Ruth wondered.

She was too tired to care. The day had been long, the miles traveled many, and the hug from Pappa secure. Crawling in under the softness and warmth, it didn't take long for Ruth to fall asleep. Tonight, there were no rats scurrying around on the floor; no soldiers outside keeping watch. Tonight, they were all together again. That was all that mattered.

Morning sunlight filled the room, shining on Ruth's face. She squinted in the brightness, trying to remember where she was. Mamma stood in the doorway, smiling at her children. Then Ruth remembered. She was in Germany, and this was Herr Lassen's house. "It's time to get up, children," Mamma instructed. "Frau Lassen has fixed a delicious breakfast, so get dressed and come downstairs. *Schnell!* [Quickly!]"

Ruth and her siblings scurried to get ready and go downstairs, where Frau Lassen and her maid served breakfast to the Reimer family. Again, Ruth found herself hoping this was real. There really were no guards barking orders. There was no shortage of food. Instead of carrying their tins and cups to the kitchen window in a camp, they were being served at the table. Everything was clean and neat. There was more than enough food on the table, and there was a place for everyone around the table.

Over breakfast, Pappa explained his plans to the family.

"I am being given time off today to go visit another family. I have talked to a lady to see if they have room for our family to live for a while. If she has room, I will take you over there to meet them."

When Pappa came back from his visit, he announced, "*Fraulein* [Miss] Märquardsen thinks they can squeeze one more family into her house if we don't mind living in small quarters."

The children smiled. They didn't mind living anywhere if they could all be together! Besides, they were used to being crowded. They had been crowded on the ferry, in barracks with thousands of refugees, and in the trucks and trains that transported them from one camp to another. To have their own place was wonderful. Besides, here they would have food to eat and a place to sleep. There would be no guards telling them what they could and couldn't do. They would be a family again!

Christina Märquardsen moved her furniture out of the rooms she provided for the family. She lived in the other side of the house with her widowed mother, and with the help of hired hands, she managed the farm on which they lived.

"Here are two bales of straw for you to sleep on until you find beds," she told the family. The Reimer family had nothing with which to set up housekeeping. There was, however, one knife that had come with Mamma and the children from Denmark. There was a Danish crown engraved on the knife. Every time the family went from one camp to another, they had to open their luggage. If the guards found any stolen items, the person would have to go back to the camp instead of leaving. No one ever found the Danish knife in all the searches, and it ended up in Germany with the family.

Frau Goseau, a neighbor who had moved to the country to get out of the city after losing her spouse in the war, had three children. She gladly shared a bed, blankets, dishes, and some food supplies with the Reimer family when she was getting ready to return to the city. Even though Frau Goseau was also displaced, she was regarded in higher esteem because she was an evacuee and not a refugee.

Fraulein Märquardsen had an attic with furniture stored in it, but she didn't offer it to the refugees. Ruth knew the furniture was there, and she often wondered if the reason the furniture was not offered to them was truly because refugees were looked down on.

Mamma and the children were used to living on very little; they hadn't eaten off plates for so many years. Pappa worked for 75 D-marks ($18.00) a month, and eventually Mamma was able to buy some plates. Later, packages from America brought some clothing as well. In time, Pappa's wages increased to 100 D-marks ($25.00) a month. Pappa and Mamma were able to borrow a table and a few chairs.

The new living quarters for the Reimer family was the downstairs part of a house. It consisted of the kitchen and one other room plus a small room under the stairsteps, just large enough for a bed. Lisa and Ruth had the room under the stairs. The common living area was the place where most of the family slept. Pappa and Mamma had a bed, Hans and Dieter slept on the couch, and Heidi slept in a crib. The kitchen was large enough to eat in, and it held a wood-fired stove. A nearby outhouse provided toilet facilities.

Another refugee family with two children lived in the upstairs of the same house. The husband was a milk inspector and therefore learned to know many farmers in the area.

Pappa borrowed Herr Lassen's team and wagon again and took Mamma with him to register for food rations. Herr Lassen paid for the electricity. Pappa worked in Dollerup for Herr Lassen who was kind to him, even though he could not pay him much in money.

"Herr Lassen will let me eat lunch at his place, and he will also provide milk, eggs, and potatoes for us," Pappa told Mamma. "I know it is not much, but we will make it."

"This is a lot more than we had in the refugee camps," Mamma replied. "Finally, the children will have milk instead of tea to drink. We will have meat, potatoes, and vegetables instead of soup and bread."

"The older children will need to help in the garden," Pappa added, looking at Lisa and Hans. "You can also help some in the fields during potato harvest. Later, you will help plant the beet and potato fields, and in harvest, you can help pick and carry potatoes after school. Hans can help with threshing."

In time, the family settled into a routine, focusing on surviving and making ends meet. Once a family who enjoyed a comfortable living, now the days were filled with pinching *pfennig* [pennies] *Deutsche* marks [D-marks] and stretching food and clothing as far as possible.

"Just think," Hans said wistfully one evening at supper, looking at Pappa. "You used to have hired men working for you on our farm. Now you are a hired hand working for another farmer."

"This is true, but I have work to do, and I can provide for my family," Pappa assured him.

"But everybody looks at us," Lisa complained. "They look at us like we don't belong here!"

"We are not from this area, Lisa," Pappa responded, "and our clothing shows other Germans that we are refugees. We are not *hiesiger* [from these parts]. Everybody has suffered because of the war, and we are fortunate to be able to find work we can do so we can be together as a family. Not many families can say they lost no one because of the war, but we can. We will count our blessings."

School days loomed ahead. Ruth had not been in school since the first grade, and now she would be in fourth grade. Hans was also in fourth grade, but it didn't seem to bother him to share a grade with his sister. Soon Hans had a lot of friends. The boys were more accepting of the new strangers than were the girls.

On Ruth's first day of school, she noticed the children looking at her strangely.

"Look at her clothes," one of the children whispered to another child. "You can tell they don't have much money."

"Must be *Flüchtlinge* [refugees]," another child responded.

"Look at her wooden shoes," a third girl whispered, pointing out the wooden clogs from Denmark.

Eleven-year-old Ruth's cheeks burned as she tried to blink back tears. She wanted to just sink into the ground. The latest package they had received from America contained one pair of shoes, but they did not fit Ruth, so she wore her wooden clogs from Denmark to her new school. Ruth's shoes still clacked when she walked, and it hurt her ankles to walk in them, but at least she had shoes!

Would she find friends, she wondered? She would never, ever forget the humiliation she felt from other children in her class on this first day of school.

Everything was new, strange, and different. Here in Dollerup in Schleswig Hostein, the children's German sounded different from hers. These children had nice clothes and shoes that fit. Yet what Ruth wore was all that her parents could afford. [Ruth never forgot how it felt to be stared at by other children. Years later, remembering that scene still brought an uprising in her stomach, and her face still burned with the shame of their hidden laughter.]

That first Christmas, Ruth portrayed the part of an angel in the school program. To her dismay, her wooden shoes clonked as she walked across the stage. Everybody heard the entrance of the angel because of her wooden shoes. Her cheeks burned with humiliation that night as she made her way onto the stage. She knew Pappa couldn't afford shoes for her, but it didn't change her feeling of humiliation.

School was held in the morning, and at noon the teacher dismissed the children for the rest of the day. Many afternoons, Mamma milked 24-34 cows each day;[31] twelve to sixteen cows for *Fraulein* Märquardsen in the morning and evening in addition to cows at a nearby farm. She was quick and efficient, and the neighbor said she was a good milker.

Mamma also hoed beets. When she came to the house in the evening, Mamma walked stiffly.

"Why are you walking so *komisch* [different]?," Dieter asked Mamma one evening.

Mamma smiled. "Oh Dieter, I have been milking cows and hoeing beets, and it makes me stiff," Mamma explained. She didn't complain. Every morning, she got up at 4 AM to limber up before she had to milk the cows again.[32]

When the children arrived home from school, Mamma was sometimes out working in a field. Before the war, Mamma had servants to help her, and the children could play without having chores to do. Life was surely different now.

---

[31] Reimer, 1.23.1951.
[32] *Ibid.*

Now Mamma was out in the barn, milking cows in the evening before suppertime. In the morning before school, she also had to milk cows, but she was back in the house to serve her family the usual breakfast of bread and coffee. The children also had to learn how to make do with what they had, especially for school.

Paper supplies were so scant that the children were happy for anything they could find on which to write. Store owners gave them old account books that had blank pages on one side. Many school assignments required a lot of writing, and paper cost ten cents a page—money the Reimers did not have.

In the afternoon after school was over and her homework was finished, Ruth and her siblings watched Dieter and Heidi while Mamma was milking. The house where they lived was small, so being outside was a respite from the crowded quarters.

"I wonder if we will ever go back to West Prussia," Lisa said. "I miss Mamma's flowers."

"I wonder what our farm looks like now," Ruth mentioned wistfully. "Do you think the Polish people who took over our farm are taking good care of it?" she added.

"We might never go back there," Lisa said. "Pappa said that our farm belongs to those Polish people now, so it isn't even ours. When Pappa has enough money, we might find a new place to live."

"That will be a long time," Hans lamented. "He has all of us to provide for, and he had to start all over. He started without anything, and everything he has now has been earned from the bottom up."

"In Denmark, we were strangers because we were not Danes," Lisa reminisced. "Here we are back in Germany, but we are still second-class citizens. The people who did not leave their homes in Germany think that they are first class and we are second class. The Germany that Pappa fought for does not exist anymore," she added. "Now we have to submit to the Occupational Forces."

"But we are receiving help from American Christians," Ruth reminded them. "They care about us. Without those bundles, Mamma said she doesn't know how we would have made it."

"At least Herr Lassen is kind to Pappa and to us," Hans wiped the sweat off his forehead. "Some farmers are mean to the refugees working for them. Herr Lassen is a nice man. We have a lot more to eat here than we did in the refugee camps!"

"Beets and turnips," Hans added. "I'm not so fond of turnips, but it beats broth with carrot peelings!"

"And then we also received those packages, like Ruth said," Lisa nodded. "That Bontrager family must be really nice people. Look at what they sent us the last time. Canned beef, flour, sugar, raisins, jam, lard, and chocolate. We never had that in the camps!"

"I wish we could meet Daniel Bontrager and his family, but we will never have a chance," Ruth said. "They live across the ocean and we live here," she added.

"Some place in Indiana, wherever that is," Hans said. "Yes, they must be nice people. They don't even know who we are, but they keep sending us packages. And finally, I'm not hungry anymore," Hans added, "We don't have as much food as we did in West Prussia, but we have enough."

"And we have each other," Lisa smiled. "Just think what it would have been like if Heidi had died in the hospital, or if Dieter had died."

"Remember how he kept asking for bread with butter and sugar?" Ruth said. "Now he can have bread with butter and sugar every day."

"Mamma always looked so sad when he asked for *brot mit butter und zucker* [bread with butter and sugar]," Lisa commented. "She couldn't give him any bread, and he was so hungry. There! That's done," she said, lifting her hoe. "Let's go inside and see if supper is ready."

The children trudged back to the house where Mamma had supper waiting for them. They could smell the aroma of fresh bread when they entered the house.

"This is so much better than the bread we had in those refugee camps," Hans exclaimed as he spread lard over his slice.

"Now don't eat so much, or you will stretch your stomach, Hans!" Lisa scolded.

"I don't care if my stomach does stretch," Hans replied, taking another bite of Mamma's soft bread. "I waited so long to have good food to eat, and I am going to enjoy it!"

Mamma smiled at her family as she took a sip of her coffee. "It is good to have food to feed my children again. I am grateful that I can work. When I was a little girl, my Pappa told me, 'It is good to learn how to work; you will always be able to use it.'[33] He was right, you know. Other girls often did not have to work in the fields, but I grew up hoeing beets, and that was hard work. You children need to learn to work, too. You will never be sorry."

While the Reimer family was struggling to make ends meet and wondering what the future held for them, others were working on finding ways to help Mennonite refugee families in Germany. One of the organizations that rose to the occasion was Mennonite Central Committee.[34] MCC had been working in Europe and especially in Germany for several years. Pastor Otto Showalter of Hamburg oversaw contacting the Mennonite refugees in the Schleswig Holstein area. Local people who cared about the plight of refugees reached out to them as well.

Later MCC asked Pappa to work with them in the distribution of goods for other refugees. Pappa spent his evenings going through the mail and opening an occasional package. He had to go places by bicycle and by train to pick up the donated supplies, and he had to pay his own train fare. Sometimes Mennonite people who lived in the area came to the Reimer home to pick up clothing, flour, and apple butter. Some of the clothing that came from

---

[33] Gingerich, p. 8.
[34] See Appendix Note.

America was second-hand. Americans were suffering from the war as well, but they continued to send items to help people they had never met, people who suffered more than they themselves during World War II.

"I think everybody who has ever known a Mennonite is suddenly a Mennonite!" Pappa told his family one evening. "Today I heard some people refer to us as the Flour Bag Mennonites!" he chuckled. "It has been quite a job to get a list of all the Mennonites in this area."

Pappa's job was to compile a list of families, including names, ages, and gender of each person—a time consuming job. Pappa was happy to help MCC with this daunting task, especially since MCC had helped them.

MCC also delivered relief to Denmark. This is how Mamma and her family had received packages while living in the refugee camps. Pappa was glad to help MCC with distribution of supplies in his area. This was a way he could return thanks for the help his family had received while they were civilian refugees of war.

Pastor Showalter of Hamburg oversaw the Mennonite refugees in the Schleswig Holstein area. Packages were sent from Mennonites in America to Mennonite refugees of war. Pappa's job was to oversee clothing distribution in the Flensburg area. He needed a place to store the items from America. When there were too many packages to store in the hallway of their house, Herr Lassen gave permission to store some packages in his barn.

Winters in this part of Germany were very cold. Summers were cool, so warm clothing and shoes were a necessity.

Pappa sat down to write to the people who were sending packages in February 1950.

> *We are grateful for the many packages that are coming to Dollerup for the Mennonite people here, and are thankful to our Lord that He has kept us healthy, and pray that God may reward you for all the good you have done for us.*

We think of you so often, and if you had not sent us all the clothing and dry goods, we would have gone down in sorrow and distress.[35]

Ruth has no shoes and my wife's are very poor. The ground here is very wet and very soft, and therefore shoes are always needed. We ask you not to send shoes with high heels.[36]

Americans did not understand that high-heeled shoes could not be worn or used. The refugees' feet had gone so long without any footwear that their feet had widened and flattened.[37] It was hard for Pappa to ask for shoes and then to specify what not to send. Yet he did that because shoes with high heels would be useless. Mamma added a few notes to his letter as well.

Everything we need is here. Like the German proverb, "Wenn die Not am groessten ist, so ist Grottes Hilfe am naechsten." [When the need is the greatest, God's help is the nearest.] I want to keep the nice cloth for myself since I have sewed for the children who are all growing taller than I am.[38]

Life for the family continued in a routine. Pappa worked long hours during the summer, and Mamma helped in the fields and on the neighbor's farm with milking. School kept the children busy in the forenoon and homework in the afternoon. They continued to scrape by, sometimes having little to eat, but still enough. Dreams of returning home to West Prussia were fading as stories from their home community came back to them. The government's prospect of giving former landowners compensation was fading. Farming was hard work, and there was no other option for Pappa.

---

[35] Reimer, Feb. 15, 1950.
[36] Reimer, *Ibid.*
[37] Gingerich, p. 45.
[38] Reimer, Mar. 5, 1950.

The House in Dollerup. Three refugee families plus Fräulein *Marquardsen, their landlord, lived in this house.*

Some evenings when Pappa was especially tired, he would reflect on his former occupation as a farm owner. "I used to think my sons would never want for work because I had two farms I would give them. Even if we could go back to our farm, I would not have the money it would take to start over now."

"I am grateful that you have work to do, and that I am able to help as well," Mamma assured him. "I can glean potatoes that are missed during the harvest. I have sewing I can do, and we are all together. When we start thinking about what we would like to have, we must remember what we do have."

"Yes," Pappa said. "We are all together, and we have each other."

"And there is no grave in Denmark holding any of our children," Mamma remembered. "I would not trade our children for more money."

Pappa smiled at Mamma. "Yes, Gerda, we must remember

to count our blessings. Even though food is more expensive again, we have help from the family in America."

"I will gladly trade coffee from the care packages to help us have eggs and flour," Mamma added.[39]

Other blessings continued to come through provisions from America. Several months later, two more packages arrived from the Bontragers. The first box included a coat for Mamma.

"Look, Hans," Mamma exclaimed as she tried on the coat. "It fits perfectly!"

Next came the shoes. A pair for each child. Such excitement as the children tried on the new shoes! The shoes fit because—at the request of the Bontragers—Mamma had traced each of their feet on the back of a newspaper that was sent to them. This is how the Bontragers knew what size to send for each of the children.[40]

Heidi danced around the room, "I like my shoes; I like my shoes!" she said.

"I can't wait to wear them to church on Sunday," Ruth exclaimed as she tried on the new shoes obviously purchased for her.

The children gathered around as Mamma opened the second package. "Look, children!" Mamma exclaimed. "Soap! Trousers for Pappa and the red soap that helps Pappa's hands. And chocolate!"

"Can I have some, Mamma?" Dieter exclaimed. "Please?"

"Me want some, too," Heidi exclaimed. "Me have some?"

Mamma smiled. "We will have to use it sparingly, for it will soon be gone," Mamma said as she handed one small piece of chocolate to each of the children.

Pappa reached for the red soap. "Ever since I am using this soap, my hands have healed and are not chapped.[41] I wonder where they get this soap," he opened the container and took a whiff.

---

[39] Reimer, May 22, 1949.
[40] Reimer, Feb. 15, 1950.
[41] Reimer, Mar. 5, 1950.

"Look, Lisa," Mamma said, pulling out nylons. "A pair of stockings for you!"

Lisa reached for the stockings, smiling. "I can't wait to wear these to church!" she exclaimed, opening the package and fingering the thin nylons.

Mamma pulled out some towels and washcloths. Next she pulled out yarn. "Now I can knit stockings and mittens for the children!" Mamma exclaimed.

"This is like Christmas in summer!" Ruth exclaimed. "And I'll have new shoes to wear. I haven't had new shoes for how many years?"

Mamma smiled. "It has been a long time, Ruth. Look at this cloth! I will use this cloth to begin sewing dresses for you girls."

"We need to write a letter to the Bontragers to thank them," Pappa said. "Let's do it now!"

> *It is almost beyond our grasp that your love for your neighbor is above everything, according as the Lord Jesus Christ taught us in Scripture. . . . It is impossible to express our thanks to you. We would be half-naked and ragged today if we would not have received the things we did. Even though most everything is available to buy, our money that we earn through hard work would never reach to make the purchase. We are asking our Father above to bless you for all the good we have from you, and that He may reward you. It is hard for us to understand how you do it.*[42]

Each refugee region had a Mennonite minister assigned to function as a regional shepherd. Many of these ministers were refugees themselves and could understand the plight of the refugees. Near the Reimer family was another Mennonite family. From time to time, the two families would gather in the Reimer living quarters

---

[42] Reimer, Nov. 11, 1949; May 28, 1950.

where Ernst Regier (a Mennonite bishop formerly from West Prussia and now over their jurisdiction)[43] gave communion to the baptized members.

Sometime later, Albert Bartel, an elder from the Danzig area, was charged with leadership over this area. Bartel himself had been a prisoner of the Russians. As more Mennonite families in the area were discovered, a church was started in Flensburg, and the congregation met every other month.[44]

As December was ushered into Dollerup, the Reimer family prepared to celebrate Christmas together. It was their first Christmas since they were free, their first Christmas where all of them were together.

The Christmas tree was an important tradition that continued this year. On Christmas Eve, the Reimers went to church at four o'clock and then ate supper together. Then they gathered in the *Stube* [living room] and listened to Pappa read the Christmas story from the Bible.

The candles flickered on the tree as excitement shone on the faces of the children. Even though they did not have much, there would be some presents and Christmas bundles, and they had each other. All of them were together.

"I remember that Hitler told Germans to get rid of the Bible. He wanted everybody to own his book, *Mein Kampf* [My Fight], and read it instead of the Bible," Pappa said as he closed the Bible and put it back on the shelf.

"It was a mistake," Mamma said sadly. "We didn't realize how wrong he was."

There was silence in the room. Ruth remembered the dismal days of the refugee camps and wondered how different her life would have been if Hitler had not come to power. *I wonder why people didn't see how evil he was*, she pondered.

---

[43] Gingerich, p. 44.
[44] *Ibid.*

"Come, children," Mamma said. "Let's sing some Christmas songs. We are all together again! Let's be happy."

They sang Christmas songs and then opened their gifts. This year, the gifts were mostly Christmas bundles from America. Each package had the words, In the Name of Christ, stamped on it and was labeled MCC.

Oceans apart, Mennonite churches and families in America prepared care packages and Christmas bundles to be shipped to refugees in war-torn Germany and Europe. The Christmas bundles were prepared by placing hygiene items inside a large towel. The towel was folded over on all four sides, sealing the soap, toothpaste, wash cloths, and toothbrushes inside. The towel was then pinned together with safety pins. Every item was appreciated and used by refugees, including the safety pins.

Ruth received other blessings as well. She received gifts from people she had helped. When Ruth's school friend Christa Thaysen broke her right arm, the teacher asked Ruth to help her with her homework. Every day after school, Ruth went to Christa's home to help her with homework. Christa's family owned a bakery. What a treat it was for Ruth to be able to eat cakes and cookies from the Thaysen's bakery while helping Christa with her homework!

This year, in addition to gifts in the Christmas bundle, Ruth received a box from the Thaysen family with a doll baby and a lot of other goodies.

"Oooohhh!," the other children exclaimed when Ruth opened the box with the goodies.

"Here, everybody gets to have some!" Ruth shared happily.

What a long time it had been since any of them had been able to have cookies and candy like this! Their first Christmas together would invoke warm memories for each of them for years to come.

On Christmas morning, Fräulein Marquardsen invited the family for breakfast. After breakfast, Ruth received another gift—a small wooden box with beautiful wood grain. This gift would travel with her to each new home.

A few days after Christmas, the Reimers received another letter from the Daniel Bontrager family, telling them that another package was on the way to them. With excitement and anticipation, the children went to bed each evening, wondering when the package would come.

Finally, on the fourth of January, the package arrived. Such excitement! Ruth's family gathered eagerly and opened the box. More food, and chocolate, coffee, and clothing!

"I don't know how to thank them," Pappa said. "We can only ask God, the Lord, to reward them for it."[45] When I write to them, I will tell them that the children were nearly out of their minds when they saw these nice things.[46]

"And I don't know how we would survive without these wonderful gifts," Mamma said. "Food, clothing, and shoes! We could never afford to buy all these things!"

The following spring, another package arrived. This one contained trousers for Pappa that fit his 6'4" frame perfectly. Again, there was the much-loved chocolate as well as soap and clothing.

"I won't need to do much altering," Mamma exclaimed as the children tried on the new clothing. "I can make this black dress fit you well, Ruth," she told her daughter.

"Look at me, Mamma!" Heidi exclaimed, twirling around in her new red dress.

---

[45] Reimer, Jan. 7, 1951.
[46] Reimer, June 23, 1951.

Mamma's eyes twinkled. "Yes, Heidi, it fits you so well. Now you have a new dress to wear!"

Pappa especially liked receiving an item he called "red soap." He explained to the Bontragers why he liked this soap so much. "I always had chapped hands," he wrote, "but since I wash my hands with this soap, my hands are healed and no longer chapped."[47]

Although the Reimer parents and grandparents had been churchgoers, the children had never attended because reverence was important in church services, and in West Prussia, children were not expected to sit still during church. Consequently, the parents and grandparents alternated Sundays; the adults who did not go to church stayed home with the children. Although the preacher read from the Bible in church, the family did not even open their Bible at home— except on Christmas Eve. Neither did Ruth's family pray before meals.

Mamma had instilled in her children the need for prayer—for Pappa, and for Heidi, and for Dieter when they were ill. The children learned poems about God and recited prayers at bedtime. Mamma had taken a songbook along when they fled to East Germany, and it remained a constant source of faith for her during her stay in the refugee camps. Because there was no Mennonite church in Dollerup, the family attended a Lutheran church where Pappa asked the Lutheran pastor if Hans and Ruth could go through classes for confirmation. It was customary for Mennonite children to be baptized after two years of *Tauf-Unterich* (Instruction for Baptism). None of the children were baptized in the Lutheran church. Lisa and other Mennonite children had been baptized by Bruno Ewert in one of the camps in Denmark. By this time, the entire family went to church on Sunday, which was a new experience for them. Ruth liked going to church with her family, and she especially liked it that her family was all together.

---

[47] Reimer, Mar. 5, 1950.

Chapter Thirteen

A Place of Belonging

November 1950 - Fall 1951

School soon became a pleasant and fun place for Ruth and her siblings. In time, they developed friendships. Even though food was not plentiful and they often did not have enough to take lunch with them to school, other children shared with them. Some children brought sandwiches to school for Ruth and her siblings. This "lunch" was called *zweites fruehstueck* [second breakfast] and was common in Germany for everyone, whether a worker or a school child. After a half-day of school, the children went home, where they completed school assignments and worked on the farm. Some days Mamma tried to teach the children more when they were not in school.

The Reimer children attended school in the next village, Grundhof, six days a week, rain or shine. It was a three-mile walk to school and, although food was still scarce, those were the best school years.

Poetry was an important part of the school curriculum. Ruth learned a poem nearly every week in school. The children stood in front of the class to recite the poems they had learned. In school, there were also religion classes once or twice a week where the children learned Old Testament Bible stories.

Games during recess included hopscotch, jump rope, and volleyball. Before the school year closed for the summer, students had a *Kinderfest* [children's party.] On this day, the children came to school dressed nicely. They played a variety of games: races, throwing balls, and jump rope competitions. Children jumped rope around

Ruth with Helga.

bottles set on the ground without hitting the bottles. A child who hit a bottle with the rope or his feet was out of the competition.

After school, Ruth enjoyed looking after Helga, the toddler born to Fraulein Märquardsen sometime after their arrival in Dollerup. Helga's grandmother watched Helga when Christina was out harvesting and threshing. By the time Ruth was home from school and it was time for "coffee," Helga was awake from her nap. Children enjoy being with other children, so Helga could often be found playing with Ruth. Because Ruth "babysat" Helga, she was invited by Frau Märquardsen to have a cookie or cake with Helga.

Near the end of the school year, Fraulein Märquardsen bought material and gave it to Ruth. Because Mamma was busy working on the farm and did not have a sewing machine, Ruth took the fabric to another lady who made it into a dress for her. Ruth had a new dress for the *Kinderfest* (children's party). Later, Christina loaned Mamma her sewing machine. This machine had to be hand-turned as one sewed. Mamma's children took turns standing next to the sewing machine turning the wheel so Mamma could sew. Mamma borrowed it for a few days at a time.

Bike Trip in 1951 with school friends.

One year, the school announced an extended bike trip. The Reimer children didn't have money for the trip, but through the generosity of others, they were able to participate. The Reimer children had one bike.

"Are you going on the bike trip?" Ruth's friend Gerda asked.

"I don't have a bike," Ruth replied. "Hans is going to ride our bike."

"We have an extra bike you can use," Gerda offered. "You can take our bike."

A warm feeling enveloped Ruth. In the past, making friends had been challenging. As a refugee, she had felt like an outcast. But the years had been kind to her in providing friends, and she would never forget Gerda's generosity in making this special trip possible.

This school bicycle trip was a time of restoration for Ruth. There were twelve students and two adult teachers, one male and one female. Each student took turns writing down what they did on the trip each day. Sometimes they camped outside or stayed in barns, and other nights they stayed in youth hostels. Much of their cooking was done over campfires. The trip lasted four weeks, and they traveled 1,000 kilometers.

The students were delighted to bike along the scenic Rhine River and see the legendary Lorelei,[48] an imposing rock formation at the water's edge. They enjoyed singing the song *Ich weiß nicht, was soll es bedeuten* as the wheels on their bicycles moved along. Sometimes they changed the words of the song to match the weather of the day.

Ich Weiß Nicht, was soll es Bedeuten
Ich weiß nicht, was soll es bedeuten,
Daß ich so traurig bin,
Ein Märchen aus uralten Zeiten,
Das kommt mir nicht aus dem Sinn.
Die Luft ist kühl und es dunkelt,
Und ruhig fließt der Rhein;
Der Gipfel des Berges funkelt,
Im Abendsonnenschein.
Die schönste Jungfrau sitzet
Dort oben wunderbar,
Ihr gold'nes Geschmeide blitzet,
Sie kämmt ihr goldenes Haar,
Sie kämmt es mit goldenem Kamme,
Und singt ein Lied dabei;
Das hat eine wundersame,
Gewalt'ge Melodei.
Dem Schiffer im kleinen Schiffe,
Ergreift es mit wildem Weh;
Er schaut nicht die Felsenriffe,
Er schaut nur hinauf in die Höh'.
Ich glaube, die Wellen verschlingen
Am Ende Schiffer und Kahn,
Und das hat mit ihrem Singen,
Die Loreley getan.

---

[48] A famous mountain along the Rhine River.

[I cannot determine the meaning
Of sorrow that fills my breast:
A fable of old, through it streaming,
Allows my mind no rest.
The air is cool in the gloaming
And gently flows the Rhine.
The crest of the mountain is gleaming
In fading rays of sunshine.
The loveliest maiden is sitting
Up there, so wondrously fair;
Her golden jewelry is glist'ning;
She combs her golden hair.
She combs with a gilded comb, preening,
And sings a song, passing time.
It has a most wondrous, appealing
And pow'rful melodic rhyme.
The boatman aboard his small skiff,
Enraptured with a wild ache,
Has no eye for the jagged cliff,
His thoughts on the heights fear forsake.
I think that the waves will devour
Both boat and man, by and by,
And that, with her dulcet-voiced power
Was done by the Loreley.][49]

One of the teachers led the way while the tallest boy in the group brought up the rear. His bicycle was loaded with equipment, including a kettle for the group. The smallest boy was second in line, and Ruth was usually third because the gears on her bicycle were smaller than those on the others' bicycles. She had to pedal harder to go the same distance. By following Ruth, the rest of the class

---

[49] This song is about the Loreley (Lorelei) legend about a beautiful maiden jilted by her sweetheart who jumped or fell into the river and died.

paced themselves with her, and this kept her from falling behind on the ride. A borrowed bicycle and other students who helped share the cost of this excursion restored her hope in people. Friends who functioned as a team by keeping her in the lead so she would not fall behind the group made her feel important and loved.

Ruth had lost so much of her childhood because of the war. In the refugee camps, she had many playmates, but it was hard to develop lasting friendships with children because one never knew how soon things would shift as the government moved families to other camps. Here in Dollerup, Ruth was finding healing and wholeness through friendships and belonging.

At long last, Ruth was beginning to feel that she belonged even though this was not her beloved West Prussia. She had friends and fun times. Perhaps there was indeed a place for her.

One of their favorite snacks was bread made wet with cold coffee and sugar added to it—just enough until it stuck. In Germany, children drink a lot of Postum. They were still poor, and they didn't always have money to buy butter for their bread, but things were better than at first.

Money continued to be tight for the Reimers, but they learned to make do with very little. After they scraped together enough to purchase some basic household goods, they could use money for other things. In time, the Reimers purchased what they needed for housekeeping. They didn't need to keep buying kitchen supplies, so they could begin to purchase other necessities. At first, Mamma could only buy one canning jar a week because she didn't have money to purchase more than one at a time. Now they owned some furniture and had household supplies for cooking and canning. They didn't need to keep buying more jars for food canning. One of Ruth's plates from West Prussia had survived the steamboat ride across the Baltic Sea, all five refugee camps, and the train ride back to her homeland. It was another reminder to her that God was providing for them.

Mamma was now able to sew some things, and the packages and bundles from America helped fill clothing needs. Pappa's legs were usually too long for the pants that arrived in packages, but he wore them anyway. Clothes did not always match, and the shoes might not have been the kind they would have chosen, but the children and their parents were grateful for every package, every bundle that came to them *In the Name of Christ* through MCC.

Even though things were better, the struggle for survival continued. One winter the Reimers could not afford to buy coal so their small quarters were cold. Pappa wrote to the Bontragers, "Heating material is in short supply. Coal is very expensive, and we cannot buy any. We go to bed early and warm each other up."[50]

The possibility of returning to West Prussia no longer held any hope since Pappa knew that Polish people had moved into his house and were farming the land. Oma Reimer had stayed at home to keep up the farm as best she could, but the Poles moved in and were not kind to her. Oma didn't have much food, so some days Oma Hintz took food to her.

Sometime later, the Russians transported Oma Reimer to an old people's home in Saxony, East Germany. When Pappa got her address, he sent food packages to her since he could not take off work or afford the trip to visit her. Oma Reimer died while in the old people's home in East Germany, and Pappa and his family never saw her after the war.

Oma Hintz fared better. In the earlier years of her marriage, Oma hosted children from the city for several weeks each summer. One of the girls, Gretchen, maintained contact with Oma Hintz. After the war, Oma wrote to Gretchen, who invited Oma to come and live with her and her family. Gretchen's husband was in the coal business and they welcomed her. The Reimer children always called her Tante Gretchen.

---

[50] Reimer, Nov. 9, 1950.

Some evenings the family talked about where they would like to live for a permanent home. It would be nice, they thought, to have a place where they could invite Oma to live with them. They had no money to invest or to start over, whether here or in West Prussia.

Some evenings Mamma and the children told Pappa about their days in the refugee camps. Pappa didn't talk much about his time in the war, but mealtimes became special times for telling stories about the war days. Sometimes Mamma and the children told Pappa about the different refugee camps they experienced. There were so many stories to tell, and Pappa wanted to hear them all.

One evening during supper, Pappa and Mamma talked about where they should move with their family.

"You have had to work so hard to provide for us," Mamma said. "How I wish we could go back to our farm and the days like they were."

"Yes, Hitler used to say there will be a chicken in every coop and a car in every shed," Pappa snorted. "We heard that slogan, 'Germany is ours today; tomorrow the world.'"

"And he said, 'It is going to be so good that you'll never recognize Germany again,'" Mamma added.

"We had no idea how true those words were," Pappa said sadly.

"We lived through World War I, and the worldwide recession made us want to believe anything would be better than what we had. We were finally coming out of the recession, and the Nazis had all these programs of how to put people to work building the autobahn. It sounded too good to be true." Pappa's voice was low as he added, "And it was."

"The main thing is that we are all together," Mamma reminded him. "So many families lost members, and our family is complete. We are blessed that not one of us died from the war or the refugee camps."

"Yes, Gerda," Pappa said. "You are right. I didn't know when I became a prisoner if I would come out alive. It was the providence of God, I know."

"You never told us much about your time in the war," Mamma said carefully.

"I want to hear about it, too," Lisa said. "We have told you what happened to us, and we want to know what happened to you." Pappa was quiet for a long time. Finally, he cleared his throat.

"This might be hard for the younger children to understand," Pappa began.

"They will be okay, Hans," Mamma encouraged him. Mamma believed that talking about the past helped them all to understand what had happened during the time they were apart. She thought it was more helpful to talk than to keep quiet about their experiences. Pappa's foot tapped the floor, and he leaned his arms on the table, staring down. He took a deep breath, took another one, and started talking.[51]

"When I realized that Germany was going to lose the war, I knew I would become a prisoner," he began. "It occurred to me that I could choose which soldiers would take me prisoner. That was the middle of April. I made my way over to where the Allied forces were fighting because I did not want to become a prisoner of the Russians."

Mamma reached for his hand. She stayed quiet and waited. This was what he had told them the day they arrived on the train. Was he ready to say more?

After a while, Pappa continued.

"On May 4, I was picked up by Allied soldiers and brought to Neuengamme Concentration Camp in Hamburg. Here I was, a soldier formerly guarding Germany's concentration camps and now I was a prisoner being guarded. That first year was torture."

Mamma squeezed his hand. Pappa's chair scraped the floor as he scooted his chair back a little from the table.

---

[51] Information about Pappa's experiences comes from the interview by Gingerich, pp. 17-26.

"Being a prisoner sure made me realize what it was like for the Jewish prisoners I guarded. I am grateful, however, that to my knowledge, I did not take anyone's life."

Pappa was quiet for a while, and the children waited patiently with Mamma. He continued. "We had to work hard and there was hardly anything to eat. Sometimes we found peelings from the trash pile and ate those. Anything was better than nothing."

Mamma and the children nodded. They knew about being hungry and finding scraps of food to eat.

"Sometimes," Pappa lowered his voice, "the officers beat us. They'd bring us in for questioning and if they didn't like my response, they'd beat me. All that time, I kept wondering if you and the children were okay, but I didn't know. I didn't know there was another baby!" Pappa's voice cracked, and he swallowed hard.

"When I first arrived at the concentration camp, they took all the prisoners out to a field and told us to stand in a circle. Then they told us to throw our watches, wallets, jewelry, and any other papers we had into the circle in the field. The soldiers built a fire in the center where they were going to burn our things."

Pappa was having a hard time talking now. The children took their cue from Mamma and waited quietly. Outside, the moon peered through the kitchen window at the family gathered around the kitchen table. Mamma knew it was hard to talk about those difficult days. She also knew that talking would help her husband and all of them. Mamma sat, waiting.

"Since I was taller, I was in the back row where the officers couldn't see me as well. I reached down into my pocket to pull out my *Soldbuch* [soldier record diary]. I was going to obey the officers and throw it into the circle. The other soldiers were pulling their books out and throwing them into the fire. But just as I pulled it out, I felt a voice say to me, 'Don't throw that in there. You will need that book. Keep it!'

Mamma's gaze shifted quickly to Pappa's face. Her lips trembled, but she didn't speak. Ruth looked at Lisa, who was watching Pappa.

"It wasn't really a voice, Gerda," Pappa said, "but it was like a voice told me that. I looked around, and I knew that nobody else heard that voice, so it appears it was just said to me. Instead of throwing my *Soldbuch* into the circle with all the other things being thrown in, I just put my hand with the *Soldbuch* into my pants. It dropped down my leg and into my high boot."

In the distance, crickets and frogs sang in rhythm to each other while the stars shone brighter in the sky. Even little Heidi sat quietly on Mamma's lap, watching.

Pappa continued. "You know I am not much of a religious man, but I know that voice I heard was from God, telling me to keep that *Soldbuch*. Gerda, I believe that *Soldbuch* saved my life."

"Oh Hans," Mamma murmured, hugging Heidi tightly, "I had no idea."

"The soldiers were mean and rough sometimes. One day an American soldier walked up to me and tore my pocket watch away from me. The chain was still dangling on my belt, so I told him, 'You can take the chain, too!'

"Later the British forces took us into their charge because the Americans retreated across the Elbe River. We were moved to Neuengamme in Hamburg. I spent one year at Neuengamme as a prisoner of war. We had interrogation after interrogation. I had no hope of being released. The Allies wanted to find out everything   possible that had taken place. I heard that those of us who belonged to the SS were in the greatest danger of a long imprisonment. I had resigned myself that it would be a long time until I would be released, if ever.

"One day in March 1946, we got word that we would soon be released from this camp. I didn't know what that meant. The British were anxious to retaliate for the bombing of their English cities. The guards used their *truncheon* [a short, thick stick carried as a weapon by an officer] to get answers from the POWs. One day they called the prisoners before the American officers, one at a time. I thought I was going to be sentenced. I was taken into the room by a guard, by myself. The guard shoved me into the room and then left. I was alone with an officer of the British Occupational Force. I was weak, thin, and shaking like a bird in a cage."

Pappa shook his head, looking off in the distance. His hands shook on the table, and his family realized he was seeing that room in his mind all over again. Then he continued.

"The officer was sitting behind his desk. He glared at me and said, "*Du Schwein Hund* [you pig-dog]." [This was a phrase the Nazis used for Jews and people who opposed the regime.] "Now the tables had turned! I was being called a *Schwein Hund*! The officer was gruff and impatient with me. He asked me how many men I killed as a Nazi soldier. I told him that to my knowledge, I did not kill anyone. I told him I was from Danzig, and Danzig had no army because Hitler took all the foreigners who were outside of the German Reich and recruited them into the SS. Therefore, I felt no guilt or responsibility for having been placed into the SS."

Pappa took a drink of cold coffee, and then started talking again.

"The officer kept interrogating me. Now he called me '*Du*' [informal you] instead of '*Sie.*'[formal you]. He asked me about my church membership; I told him I never left the church. He didn't believe me. He stood up, put his pistol and his whip on the desk, shook his finger at me and yelled, 'Prove it to me!'

"I stood there, shaking. I didn't know what to do. How could I prove to him that I was still a member of my church? Then I remembered my *Soldbuch*. Suddenly, I wasn't afraid. I felt calm. I showed my *Soldbuch* to him. He was really interested in that!

"I told him, 'I have all my information right here in my *Soldbuch*. It tells where I spent my time, my wages, commissions, my furloughs, the clothing issued to me, and anything else you need to know.' I put the book on the table.

"He picked it up and started looking through it. He took pages of notes from my passbook and kept questioning me. I was there for over an hour. I had been standing all that time.

"Once he looked up at me and said kindly, '*Setzen Sie sich, bitte*' [Be seated, please.] He used *Sie*, which he would not have had to do.] I was so surprised. He was now being kind to me. He even said "please!" I started watching him, trying to figure out who he really was.

"You know what I think?" Pappa's eyes met Mamma's. She shook her head.

"I think maybe he was not really a bona fide British officer, but an offended Jew. He could read German too well and check out the records too well to not have been acquainted with the whole system. We know that many Polish-German Jews had fled to England and were used by the British Army.

"Once he said to me, 'It is evident that you had a lot of furloughs and a lot of passes.' He was right. I had carefully recorded each leave from duty in that book.

"Then he noticed the autographed photo I had of Hitler on the cover. He said, 'Oh, you are still carrying a picture of Hitler with you!'

"I replied, 'Yes, of course. I have not altered that book one bit. There are no changes to be found in it. I have left everything just the way it was when I got it and filled out my records. You can see the signed pass and furlough permits. You can see my commissions and my rank. I have not altered one thing.'

"He took out his pocketknife, cut out the autographed picture of Hitler, and put it in his pocket. He kept going through my book and writing things down. It took him a long time!

"Then he told me, 'You can go now. Get yourself ready. You will be released the day after tomorrow. You will be free to go.'"

"He believed you?" Mamma asked, her voice incredulous.

"Yes, he believed me, and he told me I was free to go. I was so surprised that I just stood there. I decided I'd better go before he changed his mind!" Pappa chuckled. "And then I realized why I was not supposed to put my *Soldbuch* into the fire."

"I was going to be free, but I did not know where I would go. I did not know where you were or if you were even safe. I did not know what Grenzdorf looked like after the Russians came in, but one thing I did know. I now knew why I was to slip that passbook down my pant leg into my boot after I heard that voice from somewhere telling me to keep it. I found out that other prisoners who had destroyed their papers were kept in prison for another year or more. They did not have their passbook to prove where all they had been or what they had done. I believe it was the Providence of God that I kept my passbook."

"Surely it was," Mamma murmured.

Pappa continued, "Two days later, two British officers took me to Hamburg and left me off at the *Kunst Halle* [Art Building] where I was officially discharged and declassified from the rank of an SS soldier."

"What does declassified mean?" Hans asked Pappa.

"It is not an honorable discharge, but it is a total pardon from past services in the German army. I was now a German civilian again," Pappa explained. "Even though I was discharged in Hamburg, Hamburg was under the authority of the British Occupational Forces.

"I wanted to find you, but I had no idea where you were, and I had no place to go. I was a free man, but I had no place I belonged. All around me was devastation from the war. There were men, women and children digging around the rubble to see if they could find something they could use. Gerda, I remembered all the times back in Grenzdorf when hungry people stood at our door and begged for a bite to eat or a place to sleep for the night. Now I was one of them. Now I was at the mercy of the survivors of a bombed-out city, along with hundreds of other refugees looking for a place to rest and eat. I stopped at the Red Cross and gave them information about myself and my family.

"I was a beggar and a refugee with the shattered dream of Hitler's Third Reich where there would be prosperity, peace, and happiness for two thousand years to come. Before this, others were at my mercy. Now I was at the mercy of others. I didn't even know where or how to start over. I had no place to go.

"Then I remembered that there was a Mennonite Church in Hamburg. I remembered that a Pastor Showalter and a Pastor Haendiges who had visited the Danzig churches had been from Hamburg. Maybe the Mennonite pastor can help me, I thought. I asked the direction to the Altoona Mennonite Church, and I started walking and then got on the trolley. I had been given some money, and I used some of it to pay the trolley fare. People looked at me. I know I looked haggard and poor. My clothes were ragged, and I was too thin. Here I was 6'4" and weighed only 100 pounds. Some of the people on the trolley looked at me with pity and handed over some ration stamps so I could buy some food.

"When I got off the trolley, a man who had also gotten off came up to me and asked me where I wanted to go. I told him I was looking for Hamburg-Altoona Mennonite Church. The man said, 'You come along with me, first. You look hungry.' He took me into the fish store and bought a smoked herring and gave it to me. By now it was too late to go to the church, so I went to the train station where there was a refugee reception center with a soup kitchen set up. I ate some bread and drank some milk that was handed to me. After that they showed me a room that was an overnight place for refugees. I curled up on the straw on the floor and was given a blanket. I fell asleep almost right away. Here I was with no place to live and no job. I didn't know where my wife and children were or if they were even still alive."

Pappa's eyes rested on his children, one by one. His eyes were as blue as ever and his face was gentle as he smiled at them. Ruth shivered, thinking about what Pappa had been through after the war.

"The next morning, I was given rye coffee and bread to eat. Once again, I set out to find the Altoona Mennonite Church. I found the church and Pastor Otto Showalter. He said he had just recently returned from being a prisoner of war himself. His wife was not at home, but he served me a little leftover soup from lunch.

"I told Pastor Showalter everything about me and my family and asked him if he could help me find you. I asked him what I should do now. He said he could not find a place for me here or anywhere in Hamburg. It would be too difficult to find a place to stay or to find work. He suggested I go into the country and find work with a farmer, since I was a farmer by trade. Even though I had registered with the Red Cross, Pastor Showalter said it would be very difficult to locate my family.

"He said, 'There are fifteen million refugees who fled from the east, and three million more perished in the bitter cold,'" he told me. "Some found refuge in Denmark or are in some refugee camps in Germany, but if your family made it to Denmark, I may be able to help you.'

"Pastor Showalter promised to contact a professor who was trying to locate all the Mennonite refugee families and bring them together again. As I was leaving, he reminded me to let him know where I would be living so he would know where to reach me.

"Then I just started walking. After a while, a truck stopped, and the driver offered me a ride. I climbed in, and he asked me where I wanted to go.

Pappa chuckled now, remembering. "I didn't know what to tell him because I didn't know the area and I had no place to go. I just told him, 'Wherever you are going.'

"When we got to a village, I got out of the truck. Another refugee, a former German soldier joined me. We came to a village and saw a sign, "*Baeckerei, Thaysen.*" [Bakery Thaysen]

Pappa's blue eyes smiled at Ruth. "It was your friend Christa's family who owned that bakery. Bread! We were hungry, so we decided to go inside and see if they would let us have some bread. I stayed outside while the other soldier went inside. Soon he came out with a big smile on his face. He had a large loaf of freshly baked whole wheat and rye bread. The loaf had been split open by the heat of the bakery oven, but we didn't care."

"After we ate almost the entire loaf of bread, we started out walking again. I was wearing my SS uniform and he had on his

German soldier uniform. It was getting dark, and we saw lights up ahead coming from a farm house.

"We knocked on the door and were met by Herr Lassen. His wife fried up a large pan of potatoes for us, and we ate it all. After we ate, he took us to the barn and showed us an empty box stall we could use for the night. He threw some fresh straw on the floor. Before he left, he said, 'I will see to it that you find work.'

"For the first time in over a year, I went to sleep not feeling hungry. It didn't take long to go to sleep. There was no machine gun fire in the distance. No planes flying overhead to drop bombs or the screams of prisoners.

"The next morning, Herr Lassen told us that there was work for us on his farm and other nearby farms. He threw a few boards into a place in the barn and told me to build a bed with these. I took the boards, hammer, and nails and built a bed. He also gave me straw to sleep on. Now I had a job and a roof over my head. I was free! I just needed to get strong so I could work hard and find my family. I thought I would never see the day when I wasn't hungry anymore."

"I'm sure," Mamma said. "Frau Lassen told me that she could hardly get enough food in you when you first started working for them. She said you ate and ate and ate."

Pappa smiled. "It felt so good to have food to eat again. I thought I would never get full. Even though I have had to work hard, Herr Lassen treats me well. Next, I wanted to find you. Pastor Schowalter told me that he was contacted by Dr. Crous who discovered that Mennonite Central Committee had a list of all the Mennonites in Denmark. Pastor Schowalter then contacted me. That was when I first learned that we had another baby because I was told that a Mrs. Reimer with five children were living in Denmark in Camp Gedser. What a surprise!" Pappa smiled tenderly at Heidi who was sitting in Mamma's lap. She smiled shyly, kicking her feet. He continued, " I was so eager for us to get back together, but I knew it was going to take time."

"And all that time, we were wondering if you were alive," Mamma murmured. "They told us that SS men were either killed or would be in prison for life. You can't imagine how surprised I was to get that first letter from you."

"I waited and waited to hear back from you," Pappa said. "Until I got your letter, I could only hope that you were alive and wonder if all our children had survived. I tried to be careful what I wrote because I knew that the mail was opened and read. I wanted to make sure my letters were not confiscated and that you would get them.

"I thought I would never get the paperwork completed so you could join me." Pappa continued. "I made visit after visit to the mayor, asking him to sign the paper stating I could provide for you. He wouldn't sign the paper. I had all the information I needed. Everything was ready, but he would not sign that paper. He just refused to sign it," Pappa shook his head, still frustrated years later.

"Why didn't he want to sign the paper?," Mamma asked.

"I am not sure what his reason was. Maybe it was because he was an ethnic Dane and resented all the refugees in his country. There were so many other refugees that they couldn't take any more in the village. Maybe he thought he would get in trouble if my family added to the other refugees already here. I know the people really resented all the refugees. It put a burden on the state to have so many refugees. They were told they had to allow refugees to stay and give them jobs.

"What surprised me was the attitude that the farmers had toward the Danzig refugees or those from the east. The people who had once been heralded as the Reich's greatest soldiers were now called *Pollocken* [(a name for Poles)] and not considered as equal German citizens.

"But I was safe, and I was alive. I just wanted to be with my family. The mayor finally signed the paper in 1947, but that doesn't matter now. We are all together. We are all safe."

The quiet in the kitchen stayed. Everyone sat still, thinking about all the things Pappa had told them. Little Heidi had fallen asleep, and the other children were somber after hearing the many pieces of Pappa's story put together for the first time.

Outside, the sky was bright from the stars, and the moon beckoned goodnight. The quietness was pleasant and calm. So much had happened since those nights of air raids and wondering if they would be alive come morning. Now here they were, together again, safely back in their beloved Germany, even though they no longer owned a place to call home.

Pappa's words, "All together now; we are safe!" lingered in Ruth's mind as she snuggled in her bed tucked in under the stair steps next to Lisa. *Together and safe, that's the best place to be,* Ruth thought as she drifted off to sleep.

God Moves in a Mysterious Way

by William Cowper, 1777 (public domain)

God moves in a mysterious way
His wonders to perform;
He plants His footsteps in the sea
And rides upon the storm.

Deep in unfathomable mines
Of never failing skill
He treasures up His bright designs
And works His sov'reign will.

Ye fearful saints, fresh courage take;
The clouds ye so much dread
Are big with mercy and shall break
In blessings on your head.

Judge not the Lord by feeble sense,
But trust Him for His grace;
Behind a frowning providence
He hides a smiling face.

His purposes will ripen fast,
Unfolding every hour;
The bud may have a bitter taste,
But sweet will be the flow'r.

Blind unbelief is sure to err
And scan His work in vain;
God is His own interpreter,
And He will make it plain.

~ *Chapter Fourteen* ~

A PLACE IN ESPELKAMP

Fall 1951 - Spring 1955

Espelkamp *Mittwald* [in the middle of the wood]

Even though Mennonite Central Committee was providing relief with food and clothing supplies, the refugees continued to lack so much. More than food and clothing, they also needed a future hope for employment and real homes of their own. The Reimer family had almost nothing to call their own. Other people now owned the farms intended for Johannas' inheritance in West Prussia. How could the Reimer family—and others—find a way to completely start over when they had lost everything?

In the town of Espelkamp *Mittwald*, there was an ammunition arsenal that had been untouched by the ravages of war. Camouflaged so well that the Allies did not find it during their bombing missions,

it sat empty. A Swedish pastor, Birgel Forell, worked on neutral ground between German and English POWs and requested that the buildings be preserved instead of demolished. These buildings could be used as future housing for the refugees. In effect, the woods in Espelkamp said, "Give me a people who are homeless, hopeless, and weary, and I shall be to them a hope, a home, and a comfort. Here shall be built a city of neighbors, a community grounded in Christian love."[52]

Birger Forrell

---

[52] Emily Brunk, *Espelkamp* (Frankfurt, Germany: The Mennonite Central Committee, 1951) p. 13.

Beginning in December of 1948, MCC started building houses and remodeling the barrack building. MCC organized a group of PAX[53] [Greek word for "Peace"] men to give their time in constructing houses for the families who would move to Espelkamp. Pastor Plantiko and the *Baugemeinde* [government building officials] invited MCC to select ten Mennonite refugee families to settle in Espelkamp. The Reimer family was one of the families who received an invitation to move to Espelkamp.

A committee from Espelkamp and PAX visited Mennonite families in the Schleswig-Holstein area. "We are looking for Mennonite refugee families in northern Germany who would like to relocate to Espelkamp," the leader told them. "Espelkamp is a large forest with a place that was used for ammunition storage during the war; the Germans knew where it was, but the Allies never found it, so it was never bombed. After the war, the Allies planned to blow up the buildings, but a Swedish pastor felt it would be a pity to demolish them. This place that served as a place for war could become a place for peace," he said.

The PAX boys built houses for the Mennonites while living in one of the barracks. They remodeled the barracks for a church and businesses. Each family moving to Espelkamp was asked to help pay for the materials for their house and help finish the buildings that the PAX boys had built. The labor of the PAX team would be free because they were all volunteering. In time, five double houses were built by MCC and PAX for the refugee families. At first, four families were required to share each double house until more housing could be available.

Pappa and Mamma talked about it at length. Was this where they should move? They would be with other Mennonite families they knew, and they could finally have a place that was their own.

---

[53] Formed as a way for Mennonites to help rebuild post-war Europe and serve as a voluntary service option in the draft. See Appendix for more information.

There was much work to be done to prepare the buildings before people moved into the area. Pappa and Mamma decided that Pappa would visit Espelkamp and find out more about the program. If he felt like this was a good place to live, he would go help work.

In the fall of 1951, Pappa and some other Mennonite men went to Espelkamp *Mittwald* to start working on their house. Later, Hans joined Pappa to help as well. The men who came there to work each got a job and then helped work on the houses in the evenings. Hans had a job working in a factory as a lathe apprentice. Pappa worked on construction in the Espelkamp area; there was much to be done to build up after the war. Pappa and Hans lived with the PAX boys who did most of the work on the building. When Pappa arrived at the PAX Unit, he met the young Americans who were all conscientious objectors.[54] They were in Germany on a peace mission to help provide housing for refugee Mennonites. These men spoke a different language; however, here and there you could find one who could speak the low German. They learned to know the other PAX workers there.

Pappa thought these Mennonites were different. He told his family, "They sit around and read their Bibles. They go to church often. They even stop working on Wednesday to go to church in the evening. It seems strange to put the Bible before manual labor." Pappa shook his head. Where he grew up, people only went to church on Sunday morning. The Bible was never read in the home or privately except at Christmas. "The women," he continued," wear white caps on their heads. They are such different people."

Yet Pappa liked these strange Mennonites. They were different because they believed in living like the Bible said one should live. Their faith seemed to be personal, and it affected how they lived every day of the week. Men from America had come here to give their time to help provide a place for refugees. Who donates a year, or two, or three just to help others? Pappa wondered.

---

[54] A person who believes that going to war violates Christ's commands.

*Front (left to right): Oma Hintz, Heidi, Mamma, Pappa, and Dieter;
Back: Lisa, Hans, and Ruth Reimer.*

When he asked about this question aloud, the volunteers explained: "Our mission board has money donated by other Mennonite
Christians in America. Those who can't come to help give money so
others can come. We do this in the name of Christ."

In the spring of 1952, the Reimer family moved to Espelkamp
Mittwald. After a hearty meal at the PAX barrack, they were taken
to the house where they would live at Weichselgasse 4. This became
their new home. It was their first home since the family had become
separated in 1945. It had been seven years since they left their home
in West Prussia. They had lost the farm and their house, but they
were still together. This was the start of something new; finally, they
had found a place where they felt they belonged.

[Later Oma Hintz and her new husband would have moved
into the other part of their house. It was special to have Oma live near
them again.]

That first evening in their home as they sat down to eat,
Pappa told his family, "The PAX boys always pray before they eat,
and from now on, we are going to do the same."

Startled, his family looked at him, but they bowed their heads and closed their eyes as Pappa led in prayer.

This had never happened before! At home, they didn't talk much about God. While in Camp Gedser, Mamma had gathered her children together and told them to pray for Dieter and for Heidi when they were in the hospital in Denmark. They prayed for Pappa while they were separated, and Ruth remembered standing behind the door and asking God to help her on her first day of school. Yet they had never prayed together before a meal. A warm feeling slipped inside Ruth. She liked what had happened with her Pappa.

Now, Ruth was fifteen. She had passed the test to enter high school; however, Pappa did not have enough money to send her, so she did not go. Since she could not go to high school, she was required to go to a vocational-type school in another village and take classes. One of her courses [which today would be called home economics] required her to compile recipes in a book. Her handwriting

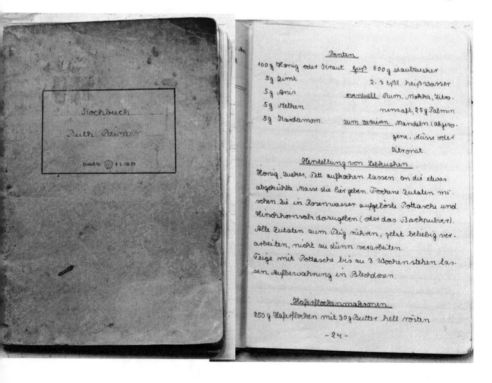

was neat and meticulous. Ruth got a job in a furniture factory, and when that factory closed, she went to work in a weaving factory. She was tired of wearing her brother's hand-me-down shoes and was glad to have some money to buy her own shoes. Next, she got a job in a family's knitting shop called Zemelka. Here they sold their own products. In this factory, they made fine sweaters. It felt good to have her own job.

Now she could buy a few items of clothing she really needed instead of wearing her siblings' worn out ones. Money was still tight, and she only purchased things that were necessary, but next she saved money to buy a bicycle to ride to work. While Ruth had friends who could buy items on credit, Ruth's parents did not allow that. The Reimer children had to save their money and pay cash for anything they bought.

Hans continued with his job in the factory. Pappa kept his job with a building firm until it shut down because of cold weather in January 1953. Prices continued to be high.

Pappa needed to work sixty hours a week[55] to make payments on the thirty-year mortgage on his house each month. One and a half hours of labor provided enough income to purchase a loaf of bread;[56] two hours of labor provided one pound of pork;[57] and one hour of labor provided two pounds of sugar.[58]

In Espelkamp, there were no Sunday school classes in the Sunday morning church services, but children's classes were held every Saturday afternoon at the *Mennoniten Heim* [Mennonite Home]. There were also Bible classes on Saturday afternoons. Sunday School was held on Sunday afternoon by the German Mennonite church. Dieter and Heidi rarely missed a class.

Mennoniten Heim was the name of Johnny Gingerich's place and was one of the barracks that had been remodeled into a house.

---

[55] Reimer, Jan. 11, 1953.
[56] Ibid.
[57] Reimer, Jan. 25, 1954
[58] Reimer, Dec. 26, 1953.

The Reimer family outside their home in Espelkamp.

The Reimer children often stopped there to play and to help take care of their chickens. Now nine years old, Dieter enjoyed feeding the chickens owned by Uncle Johnny and helping to catch the rats that were eating the chicken feed.

Church was held in one of the barracks that had been remodeled into a sanctuary. An old pump organ was part of the

The church at Espelkamp.

church furnishings, but it was not in good condition. The refugees attended another church when the pastor was not there. This was different from church in West Prussia where small children did not attend church.

After the work of the PAX boys was done, most went home. They had accomplished what they had come to do. Espelkamp, once a place used for the war, had become a place of refuge and peace. Other Mennonite missionaries stayed because of their concern for the people who were depending on church membership and good works as a means of salvation.

Christmas in 1952 was special for the Reimer family. This was the first Christmas in their new home. Lisa, Hans, and Ruth were active in the youth group. That year, the youth group produced a Christmas play. Ruth got to play the part of the innkeeper's wife who sent Mary and Joseph away.

The Reimer family had built their own Christmas Eve traditions in years past, and these traditions continued in their new home. After the church service on Christmas Eve, the family had supper. They gathered in the *Stube* [room] where real candles on the tree were lit, and Pappa read the Christmas story. After that, the family sang together before they opened their gifts. One of Ruth's favorite songs was *Stille Nacht* [Silent Night]. In Germany, there was no Christmas caroling, but the youth often went to friends' houses on Christmas day and again on December 26, which was the Second Christmas Day in Germany. At their friends' houses, they enjoyed singing Christmas songs together.

Since so many Mennonite families had moved to Espelkamp, the youth group was large. They celebrated birthdays together and experienced camaraderie. Later they had Bible studies, singings, and young people gatherings—something new to Ruth and her family. There were plenty of programs taught by American missionaries that they could attend. Sometimes they went on outings as a group, most of the time on bicycles.

Ruth

During those first years in Espelkamp, Lisa met a young man, Horst Holz. Soon another change took place for the Reimer family when Lisa and Horst got married and moved into their own home in Espelkamp. Now Ruth was the oldest daughter at home.

As Ruth listened to teaching and came to understand more and more of the Word of God, she became convicted. Her struggle was intense. She realized she was a sinner and would have to repent and give her life to Christ to ever be happy. It seemed to be impossible, and she tried to push these thoughts away. The cost of following Christ seemed to be so great. To act and do differently than she and her friends had been doing would not be easy! It would mean that her parents, brothers, and sisters would not understand her. Being a born-again Christian was quite unpopular and even unheard of by some of her friends. Others thought that being a born-again Christian was "extra religious." To become a Christian would mean hard trials!

I'll just try to live a good life and make a decision for Christ when I am older, she tried to convince herself, *but it will be easier now to become a Christian instead of fighting it so much.*

Ruth experienced the patience of a loving Heavenly Father. During a week of revivals, the minister announced that the next evening he would give an invitation for salvation.

In a deliberate decision the next evening, Ruth stayed home. *If I just stay at home, then I won't be convicted,* she told herself.

On her return to church the following evening, she was surprised to hear the minister give an invitation again! The Holy

Spirit was still working in her heart, and she gave her life to Christ. Ruth was sixteen years old.

One would think that after all Ruth had endured, life would now become easier. It did not. Now that she had come to real faith, along came the real trials. Where in the past, she had experienced loss of home, illness, and malnutrition, now she experienced other emotional and spiritual battles.

"You are crazy to go to Bible Hours," her brother-in-law said. When Ruth refused to do some things that others were doing, her brother Hans told his friend, "Ruth is a religious nut now, too."

Despite the times of discouragement, Ruth also experienced fellowship with other Christians and was strengthened by their faith and prayers. She soon developed convictions on how to live the Christian life, to leave the world, and become conformed to Jesus; she chose to take up the cross and follow Him.

Ruth, her brother Hans, and another girl were baptized by (Elder) Albert Bartel on July 27, 1952. They were the first persons baptized in the Mennonite Church in Espelkamp. For church, people dressed in their Sunday best. For special Sundays such as communion, baptism, and funerals, they almost all dressed in black. For Ruth's baptism, she wore a black dress that was made special for this occasion. She also wore a new pair of shoes from the Bontrager family.[59]

The church fellowship was special to Ruth. She really enjoyed the large youth group as they met to celebrate birthdays. Every single youth came to the youth meetings. Later, as new believers wanted to learn more about God, there were Bible studies, singings, and other programs taught by the Mennonite missionaries. Before Espelkamp, Bible studies were uncommon to Ruth and her family.

Outings were special for Ruth, and most of these were done on bicycle. Living in Espelkamp brought greater health, new friendships, and renewed spiritual health.

---

[59] Reimer, June 23, 1951; Apr. 4, 1952.

Espelkamp youth bicycle outing.

The Reimer family again received a package from the Bontrager family for Christmas 1954. A pair of shoes for Pappa in his exact size sure delighted him. "It has been eight years since I have had new Sunday shoes," he exclaimed.

"And I can sew more dresses with these yard goods!" Mamma smiled happily, fingering the fabric. "They just keep giving to us. Not only do the items they send us cost money, but just the postage itself is an enormous amount," she added.

Even so, the Reimers wanted to help give to others. Through their church in Espelkamp, they participated in sending small packages to the East Zone for Christmas.[60]

Christmas in Espelkamp was better than it had been in Dollerup. There was more money, so Mamma made a gingerbread house with a lot of candy on it. The candy could be broken off after Christmas. With a little more money on hand, the gifts were more as well. The family found comfort in the routines of their Christmas

---

[60] Reimer, Dec. 27, 1954.

The Reimer home in Espelkamp.

Eve traditions: church, supper, candles, Christmas story, songs, and gifts.

On Christmas morning, the church held a service. Christmas Day was called *Erster Weihnachts Tag* [First Christmas Day]. On the day following Christmas—*Zweiter Weihnacht Tag* [Second Christmas Day]—another church service was held.

Christmas was special for more reasons than just being together with her family. Now Ruth could also claim the Baby of Bethlehem as her Savior and her Lord.

After so many years of feeling displaced, Ruth was finally able to feel that she belonged. She had new roots, and they were growing and producing fruit. Her entire family experienced the joy of hard work and its benefits. As the family settled into living in Espelkamp, Pappa worked hard to make use of the lot they owned on Weichselgasse 4. Each lot was one-fourth acre, planned and used fully to meet their needs. Pappa dug out stumps in the lot and cut wood into even pieces. He stacked all the cut wood neatly into piles seven-feet high. Every corner of their lot was used. There was ample space for a garden where Pappa planted trees: apple, pear, plum, and cherry. He trimmed all the trees properly for maximum production. Grapes grew on carefully tended vines. The family sold surplus fruits and Mamma canned strawberries, raspberries, and currants. Pappa's knowledge of farming and Mamma's training in housekeeping stood them in good stead as they strove to make the best use of their time, expertise, and property.

The Reimers also raised pigs, chickens, and geese. In the spring, Pappa bought two baby pigs from a farmer and gathered garbage to help feed them. In the fall, he sold one pig to cover the expenses; the other was butchered for their own use and preserved by canning and smoking. Mamma had a flock of chickens for her own use; she liked to have eggs for cooking. If there were extra eggs, she sold them individually and not by the dozen. In the spring, everyone helped plant the garden. They planted no sweet corn, and tomatoes did not do well because the season was so short, but other vegetables produced abundantly. Pappa also bought goslings in the spring and fed them through the summer. He butchered the first goose for *Erntedank Tag* [Harvest Thanks] on the first Sunday in October. He butchered the second at Christmastime and sold the third to help cover expenses. As soon as the garden was harvested, Pappa planted grass and rye for pasture for the geese. When he came home from work, Pappa put the geese outside to pasture and left them out until dark. Using a dust pan and broom, he swept the droppings and put them on the manure pile because the geese would not eat the grass where the droppings lay.

Mamma taught her children to work hard and make do with what they had. They learned to be resourceful. Mamma knit socks that could last for many years. When company visited, the women continued their knitting. While the refugee families were exerting their expertise to carve out a new home with every minute's effort, they reminisced about the *Heimat* [Homeland] and the disappointing decision made at Yalta[61] by Roosevelt, Churchhill, and Stalin. That decision gave their farm to Poland without any compensa-

---

[61] Held in Feb. 1945 between Churchill, Stalin, and Roosevelt, the leaders agreed to demand Germany's unconditional surrender and began plans for a post-war world.

tion to them. As knitting needles stitched socks and garments into shape, conversation often turned to their collective memories and commiseration with fellow refugees about what had happened in the past. Discussions about communism ensued; what was done was done, and they reckoned that they did not know all the facts, nor would they ever know what all had really happened in their country during this war. Memories were repeated again and again with fellow refugees. Conversations and memories flowed, and the refugees were always thankful that they had survived the war, remembering those who did not. They were learning to be homemakers again. They were learning to live and survive in a new place. They were finding healing at Espelkamp.

In Espelkamp, the Reimers found it possible to do more than just survive. They were grateful to have a place to call their own, a place to grow much of their food, and a place to experience friendships with other believers. Church was now a community where adults and children alike worshipped and participated in services. This, too, was new and different for the Reimer family. For Ruth, who had never attended church as a child and had now made a commitment to Christ, experiencing the blessings of church was new and special. Would Espelkamp always be her home?

~ Chapter Fifteen ~

A PLACE OF RESTORATION

Spring 1955 - June 1958

Across the Atlantic Ocean and 4,000 miles from Espelkamp in a small western Maryland town, twenty-year old Kenneth Yoder decided to give up farming and spend two years in Germany to help bring post-war restoration. The decision did not come easily for him. He grew up in a large family on a dairy farm that had been in the family for generations. He planned to be a farmer, too.

Then, in rather mysterious ways, God changed his course. This was not an easy or a quick process, but there were things in Kenneth's past that prepared him for a different kind of harvest.

In addition to farming, Kenneth liked his church and connected well with his youth group. His family—including grandparents and many cousins—was well-rooted in this rural community. As the fourth child in a family of ten, he knew his help was appreciated and needed on the family farm. But relief work was not altogether foreign to Kenneth. His Great-Uncle[62] was instrumental in helping start MCC, and Kenneth was aware of the PAX program because he had heard Uncle Alvin speak about his experiences in Europe following World War I. Kate Miller, a cousin and special friend who was twenty years his senior, lived next door to the Yoders with her father. Kate's interest in relief and missions left an indelible impression on Kenneth at a young age.

As a child, Kenneth started reading his father's copies of *The Baltimore Sun*, a daily paper. What was happening in Europe during

---

[62] See Appendix.

this time fascinated him. Sometimes he found unfamiliar words. He saw one of those words so often that he finally went to the dictionary to learn its meaning. Now he knew what "camouflage" meant!

"Those Nazis sure are some smart people," he told himself. "They can paint something to disguise it and nobody can even find it from the air."

Another word that sent Kenneth to the dictionary was "refugee." His mother, Martha, was president of the church's Sewing Circle [called simply the Sewing by church members]. As a child, he heard conversations about the relief work that the Sewing was doing, and the need for help in countries following the war. The Sewing made comforters for relief. When many comforters were ready for knotting, the youth had a "comfort knotting" in the church basement. As many as twenty or thirty comforters were knotted as the guys and the girls used large needles with yarn to bind the tops to the bottoms of the comforters. Youth and children alike helped package items in bath towels for relief. Even elementary-aged children helped by sticking large safety pins into the towel flaps, securing the packages.

Men were as involved in relief assistance as the women and children. Kenneth's father, Alvin, supported relief by helping with meat canning that took place in the local community for MCC. Thousands of refugees benefitted from this annual project. The combination of his church and family's interest and support of relief modeled caring for the suffering, including refugees.

One afternoon in the summer of 1954, twenty-year-old Kenneth was driving a borrowed Farmall H tractor to mow hay in a back field on the farm. As he made round after round in the field, he felt a sense that God was speaking to him. There was no voice and no revelation, just the sense that farming was not what God had for him. The thought kept coming into his head and stayed with him as he mowed hay.

This is crazy, he thought to himself. *I feel so mixed up and confused. I thought I was going to be a farmer, but I can't get this idea out of my mind that God might have something else for me.*

He found himself arguing, *What is wrong with farming?!*[63]

As the Farmall turned the corner in the field, Kenneth remembered a most meaningful song he had chosen to lead in a music class at church: *God Moves in a Mysterious Way.*

This idea of missions surely seemed mysterious! It was not something that he had thought of doing in the past. This was not the way he had envisioned his life would go. Kenneth struggled with the sense that God was calling him to a mission field instead of the hay fields. By the time he returned to the farm that evening, the field was ready to be raked, and he was ready to find out for certain if God was calling him to something different.

A conversation with his pastor came next. Kenneth approached him and asked his advice on this different purpose in his life.

"Has anyone talked to you about this?," the pastor asked the young man.

"No one has, but I felt I should look into this," Kenneth replied.

His pastor smiled. "One of the mission board members asked me if I thought you would be open to an invitation to serve in Germany."

Kenneth was stunned, yet he reckoned with the fact that God's ways are higher than ours. If the mission board was considering asking him to serve in Germany, then perhaps this was an open door through which he should walk. Was this a confirmation of the sense of call he experienced on the tractor as he mowed hay?

In less than a year, Kenneth had his paperwork in order to do his I-W service[64] in Germany. He took classes in German at

---

[63] Yoder conversation, Jan. 15, 2019.

[64] Pronounced "One—W." This is an alternative to the draft for conscientious objectors; see Appendix.

Eastern Mennonite College in Harrisonburg, Virginia, to help prepare him for the German culture and language he would encounter overseas. Kenneth was sponsored by his conference mission board but would also help with the PAX program in Espelkamp, Germany. His family said tearful goodbyes as he set sail on the *SS Groote Beer* for war-torn Europe to serve as a volunteer for two years with only his room and board provided. Just getting there would take twelve days.

On this ocean-trip, Kenneth ate a six-course meal for the first time in his life. Quickly discerning what silverware to use for which course was an introduction to the fast pace of learning Kenneth would experience as he lived in a foreign country. He celebrated his twenty-first birthday in the middle of a bad storm at sea. The young man who had grown up in a close-knit community discovered on that journey how important it was to have a spiritual anchor and commitment to being faithful to his calling and to his God.

Before his decision to go to Germany, Kenneth's focus was on being a farmer. Now here he was, halfway across the Atlantic, leaving behind the harvesting of crops and hoping to help produce harvest in the name of Christ. On the evening of his arrival in Espelkamp, he attended a choir practice for a small group of young people where Ruth Reimer and her friends participated.

To help with his grasp of the language, Kenneth started keeping a journal in German. He spent time chronicling and describing events as well as the people in his new community. One evening he wrote, "Ruth seems to be a level-headed and sensible kind of girl."[65] Through the next few years, Kenneth observed the quiet commitment of this young girl and grew to appreciate not only Ruth, but her family as well. Ruth's siblings, Dieter and Heidi, were active in children's classes, and Kenneth noticed their exceptional behavior.

---

[65] Yoder, Dec. 24, 2018.

The Weichelgasse *in Espelkamp.*

There were now five double houses built by the PAX boys in Espelkamp. They were located on a dead-end street named *Weichselgasse* [Vistula Alley.] A footpath led from the back end of the street to the Mennonite Church, and the Mennonites frequently used this path.

To encourage town folks to keep their places looking nice, an annual competition was held. The owners of the houses in the Weichselgasse worked diligently to keep their properties in top shape. This section at Weichselgasse often won the annual prize.

Many people walked through Weichselgasse to see this beautiful street. On Sunday afternoon walks with other PAX fellows, Kenneth and his friends found their way down Weichselgasse. To get from Mennoniten Heim to the church, they went through the woods and past the Reimer home. It was a short cut, and the view was relaxing and delightful.

Sometimes Ruth was watching when the men came by. She was happy when Mamma invited them in for coffee. Mamma pitied the men because she knew they did not have coffee and cake at the Mennoniten Heim on Sunday afternoon. Did Mamma notice the sparkle in her daughter's eyes when Kenneth was near? Almost without exception, the young men received an invitation to come in for coffee and cake when they were in the area, and they were willing to oblige.

In Espelkamp, Kenneth worked for an evangelical Lutheran church for 35 hours a week in addition to teaching Bible classes and children's classes at Mennoniten Heim and two other locations. He was kept too busy to think about romance, and he knew that the PAX program strongly discouraged men from becoming romantically involved with girls while serving their time overseas. He committed himself to following this guideline.

At the end of Kenneth's two years of working under the mission board, he began working in the PAX unit with 20 other young men at Bechterdissen (another Mennonite settlement that PAX boys built, about 60 kilometers from Espelkamp). He rode his bicycle back to Espelkamp for the weekend and then returned to Bechterdissen for the following week. Because his mission was to serve others, he strove to maintain friendships with both guys and girls alike, making certain that he did not lead girls to think he had romantic intentions.

Kenneth stayed one year longer to continue working under the Conservative Mennonite Conference to help build a new house and chapel in Espelkamp. When MCC made reservations for the young men to return to America via ship, Kenneth planned to be on board that ship and go home. The last day he could cancel his reservation fell on a Catholic holiday, and the young American decided to go into town to watch the celebrations and sort things out in his mind.

At the same time, a group of young Beachy Amish guys from Berlin (Germany) asked him to give them a tour of the surroundings. Since he was fluent in the German language and had been in the country for three years, they knew he would be a good tour guide.

"I can't go with you," he told the guys. "I have an important decision to make, and I need time to pray about this."

Hearing Kenneth's yearning, another young man in the group offered to join him. After spending the morning talking and praying, they walked uptown to watch the events and the parade. While there, John Gingerich, the leader at Mennoniten Heim, came to find Kenneth.

"I need to talk to you," John said. "I just got a call from MCC asking about an international work camp; everything had been arranged, but then their location fell through. They want to know if they can send their group to work at Espelkamp instead. I told them we have work that needs to be done, but I can't do the work myself. If you are willing to stay and help, I will tell them to come."

Suddenly, it seemed the pieces had fallen into place. Kenneth remembered the sense of call in his father's hayfield several years before. Instantly, he felt he knew what he should do.

The unrest in Kenneth's mind left as he told John, "Tell them to come. I will stay."

Instead of boarding passage on that ship back to America, he stayed longer. Kenneth knew the answer was right, but still there were questions. Here he was. More time in Germany. More time in Espelkamp. What did God have in mind for him? He had been looking forward to going home, and he knew his family hoped he would return home, but God had plans for him here. This was serious business. What plans did God have for him?

During those first years of this PAX man's time in Espelkamp, Ruth continued to grow and mature. Her involvement in church played a key role in her development. She was elected to the Youth Committee and taught Sunday school. She participated in the church youth group and helped sing in groups for special occasions.

Life was different now from when she lived in the refugee camps. Housekeeping and cooking were not easy to learn in the camps, and now she was learning what it was like to live a normal life. There, survival was the goal. Here, she thrived as she developed friendships and helped in the programs at Mennoniten Heim. After those years of hunger, want, and not belonging, Ruth had matured into a lovely young lady.

Ruth's new home and church in Espelkamp had introduced her to a genuine relationship with God. She experienced and delighted in the restoration of her family. Most especially, she delighted in the restoration she had found in her soul.

~ Chapter Sixteen ~

A PLACE FOR ROMANCE

June 1958 - February 1960

Ruth's genuine commitment to God and involvement in her church did not go unnoticed by Kenneth, who began asking God what plans He had for him now that he was staying in Germany. He had fulfilled his time overseas, but here he was. Did God have another purpose?

After this decision to stay in Germany, Kenneth took even more note of Ruth. He reasoned that perhaps this was one reason he was staying longer in Germany.

And Ruth? She had noticed Kenneth and respected his commitment to Christ, but he was American. She thought he was going back to America, and she would not see him again. Now things had changed, and maybe she could allow herself to care for him.

To his delight, Kenneth discovered that Ruth was open to pursuing a relationship with him. He smiled to himself when he realized that she was maybe a step or two ahead of him even though she had never displayed that interest. Ruth was not surprised when he asked her for a date. In Germany, a date usually involved going on a walk or to an activity with others. On this evening in June 1958, they walked to a Lutheran church to see a film, since there was no church service at Mennoniten Heim. Ruth had not told her best friend that she had a date, nor were the other youth from Mennoniten Heim aware. Some of her friends came later, and to Ruth's chagrin, they stopped to talk to the couple when they came past their pew to their seats.

During the rest of the summer and autumn, Ruth and Kenneth spent time together, learning to know each other, and talking about

Ruth on a date with Kenneth in his bug.

A date in Holland with Kenneth's new car.

their different cultures. The possibility of moving to another country so far away from her parents was not a problem for Ruth. In leaving her homeland and living in another country as a foreigner, was God preparing her for another move sometime in her future?

When Kenneth prepared to return home in November of that year, it was a bit harder to go back to America. Ruth and Kenneth had talked of marriage, but there was no engagement because they realized there were some hurdles to cross first.

After Kenneth returned to America, he and Ruth corresponded regularly via air mail. They not only shared what was happening in their lives, but also the struggles they faced. In one of her letters, Ruth told her boyfriend about the nights she cried into her pillow because of the ridicule she experienced from other young people who did not share her call for commitment to Christ. Living in the refugee camps and being away from her homeland had been difficult, yet here she had trouble of a different sort. She turned to the young man who had become her confidant and her friend and poured her heart out to him in her letters.

Over the next year, letters written in German crossed the ocean miles as Kenneth and Ruth continued to correspond. On his side of the ocean, Kenneth also had difficulty. His parents had concerns about the relationship their son had developed with the German girl they had never met, and asked their son's permission to write to Ruth. She was young, and the change in culture would be dramatic. Was she ready for this type of commitment? Would she be able to leave her homeland and make America her home for life if this was where God called her to live? Ruth responded to their questions with directness and kindness. Again, her commitment to Christ came through in her letters, and Kenneth's parents gave their blessing on a forthcoming marriage.

Finally, Kenneth returned to Germany on December 15, 1959, to visit his Ruth and her family again. He had not told Ruth that he was returning to Germany with the intent to ask her to be his bride. In keeping with German tradition, their courtship was kept low-key. Kenneth wanted to get better acquainted with the Reimer family and work at Mennoniten Heim, and help with construction and other upkeep of the buildings.

Initially, when Kenneth and Ruth talked about the possibility of marriage, they thought Ruth would come to America, learn to know his people, and see if she could adjust to living there away from her family. To their dismay, they learned that it would take two to three years to obtain a VISA because Ruth was born in Nazi Germany. However, if she came as the wife of an American citizen, she could come right away.

After spending three years in Germany, becoming fluent in

the language, and learning to understand the culture there, Kenneth was not concerned about adjusting to life in Germany. Farming didn't seem as important now as he reckoned with the call of God on the life he was choosing with Ruth. Kenneth told his fiancé that he was willing to live in Germany if she decided she did not like living in America.

"I like this country, and I could live here," he assured Ruth.

Engagement Day photo.

Their engagement took place in January. Usually engagements warranted much celebration. Cards and gifts were given to the

Photo taken on their engagement day.

Wedding photo.

happy couple and a party was held. While engagements often lasted several months or more, theirs would only be a two-month engagement as the wedding date was set for March.

In keeping with German tradition, the wedding was not announced until two weeks prior to the civil ceremony. Having registered at the courthouse in Espelkamp, their names were posted on the bulletin board outside the courthouse. Passersby could view the bulletin board and read the names of those waiting to be married. In Espelkamp, it was another cold day on March 5, 1960. The street in front of the German Mennonite Church was muddy. John

Gingerich drove Kenneth Yoder's black VW Bug over to the Reimer home. Pappa and John Gingerich were the witnesses for the civil ceremony. Kenneth and Ruth sat on the back seat of the Bug while Pappa and John Gingerich drove to see the Justice of the Peace for the couple to be married by the civil court. Following the legal ceremony, the justice opened his large record book and inscribed their names in the book, and the bride and groom added their signatures.

After the 11:00 AM civil ceremony, the couple returned to Espelkamp. At three o'clock in the afternoon, the brick barrack Mennonite Church began to fill with guests. The service[66] began at 3:30 PM. Pastor Albert Bartel, who had baptized Ruth, had the message. His theme was Proverb 3:5 and 6.

> *He that carried yesterday*
> *He that holds today*
> *He that will have tomorrow in His hands,*
> *His grace be with us all,*
> *Jesus Christ, the same yesterday,*
> *Today, and forever. Amen.*

Throughout the message, the emphasis was on this scripture: *Verlass dich auf den Herrn von ganzem Herzen, und verlass dich nicht auf deinen vertand; sondern gedenke an Ihn, in allen Deinen Wegen: So wird Er dich recht fuehren.* [Trust in the Lord with all your heart and lean not on your own understanding; in all your ways submit to him, and he will make your paths straight. Proverbs 3:5-6]

"And this is not the first time, my dear bride, that you hear this Word spoken from my mouth. Yes, it was on that mid-summer day, when you with us were assembled for our first baptismal class, there in our young fledgling church, and I was privileged to spread my hands over your head and give you this verse on your way, *Verlass dich auf den Herrn.* [Trust in the Lord with all your heart.]

---

[66] Gingerich, pp. 52-55.

"And so you (Kenneth) will not find it easy to leave us here and say farewell. You too have deep roots among us. *Verlass dich ganz auf den Herrn.* [Trust in the Lord with all your heart.] Everything that you may find difficult, if it is enlightened by His godly light, then you will find power enough to carry that heavy load together with Him."

After the congregation congratulated the newly married couple, the invited guests made their way to Weichselgasse 4 to be received in the Reimer home for coffee and cake. Because of the wishes of Kenneth and Ruth, the usual flow of alcoholic beverage was omitted. The "coffee" was at 4:30 PM. There was a lot of visiting and reminiscing around the table and outside the house until 10:30 PM, when a full course meal was served. Harvey Miller, missionary to Luxembourg, then shared a talk after supper. Harvey was a cousin of Kenneth's father and the only family member of Kenneth who attended the wedding.

So much had happened since the day Ruth fled her homeland in April 1945. She and her family had survived the war and had managed with hard work on their part and the help of God's people, to make Espelkamp their home. From one situation to another, Ruth could trace the hand of God in her life. When she lived in Denmark, all she and her family wanted to do was to return home to West Prussia. That dream was never fulfilled. Yet God had moved in mysterious ways to bring her to Espelkamp, where she met her future husband.

Now Ruth and her new husband would begin another journey; she would leave her homeland to travel across the Atlantic. Unchartered waters lay ahead, but she was trusting the same God who had carried her through the years of war, separation, and rebuilding. She knew that in her new country, He would continue to direct her path.

Thirteen days after their wedding, Kenneth and Ruth said goodbye to family and friends in Espelkamp. Well-wishers came to see them off and bid farewell with hugs and some tears. Mamma's tears were also evident as she hugged her daughter goodbye.

As Pappa shook his new son-in-law's hand, he said, "Keep your head up." It was his way of saying, "No need to cry."

The ship Maasdam *that Kenneth and Ruth sailed on to America.*

The newly married couple traveled to Holland to board the ship *Maasdam* that would take them to America. The VW bug was loaded. In addition to the essentials that Ruth brought with her were several treasures. The tiny wooden box she received from her landlord Christina Märquardsen was wrapped snugly inside her suitcase. Nestled with care was one plate left of the set that she and Lisa had packed the morning they left West Prussia for Denmark. This one surviving plate was traveling home to America with Ruth. Her sewing machine was strapped on top of the car. Along the way, they had to stop and weld the legs of the luggage rack because of the heavy load.

On Saturday morning, March 19, 1960, Ruth looked backward toward the European shores as the *Maasdam* sailed up the river to cross the English Channel and then headed out into the Atlantic. When the *Maasdam* docked in the New York harbor, she would be welcomed on American soil. Holding her torch high, the Statue of Liberty welcomed Ruth and her shipmates. Ruth didn't know what life would be like in this new world, but she knew God would direct her paths, just as He had done all her life so far. She was committed to her husband and to her new life in America.

~ *Chapter Seventeen* ~

A PLACE TO CALL HOME
March 1960

Ruth did not know that she would receive a warm welcome from her new husband's family as well as from those in her new community in western Maryland. She also could not begin to fathom the adjustments into the American, English-speaking culture. Her heavy accent tickled innocent little girls who surrounded her after church and asked her questions just so they could hear her talk. When she responded in broken English, they giggled and ran away.

What Ruth did know was that God had ordered her path, and mysterious as though it seemed at times, she would continue to trust in the Lord. His providence and care had kept her safe as she sailed with her family on a steamboat while enemy planes attacked from the air. He had kept her and her family safe in five refugee camps in Denmark. He had provided a way for her family to be reunited and make a home in a different part of their homeland.

The brilliant sunset was slowly fading above the western Maryland hills as Ruth and her husband arrived in her new community on March 30, 1960. Her husband's family awaited there eagerly to welcome her. Ruth knew with certainty that God had ordered her steps, and He would guide her in her new life, her new home. She was oceans away from her birthplace in Germany. Yet God was with her today, just as He had been in her past. Here, in America, Ruth had finally found a place to call home.

Ruth and her siblings (Lisa, Dieter, Ruth, Heidi, and Hans) when they enjoyed ten days together in Grantsville, Maryland.

Epilogue

• Ruth celebrates her birthday in July 2019—82 years after her birth this printed story continues to chronicle the faithfulness of God. She and Kenneth live on the home farm in Grantsville, Maryland, where they raised two sons and five daughters. They have 12 grandchildren and six great-grandchildren.

• In 1962, Kenneth was ordained to the ministry in the Conservative Mennonite Conference.

• Pappa Reimer died in 1987.

• Mamma Reimer died in 1995.

• In 1996, all of Ruth's siblings came to America for ten days to visit Ruth and her family. During their visit, they had an impromptu family photo taken (on previous page). It was the last time all the siblings were together.

• Ruth's brother Hans died in 1997.

• Ruth's brother Dieter died in 2012.

• Ruth's sisters, Lisa and Heidi, are still living in Germany. Lisa still has the autograph book she made in the refugee camp in Denmark.

• Ruth never went back to West Prussia to visit her childhood home. Some of her siblings, as well as her mother, returned to visit and were dismayed at the disarray of their house and farm. Although Ruth had the opportunity, she chose not to return to visit. She said every time she considered going back, she had nightmares.

• The young boy Heinz was never heard from again. Because his wounds were so severe, it is assumed he died in the Denmark hospital or before he made it to the hospital.

• Pappa and his family never saw Oma Reimer after they fled Germany, and she died in an old people's home.

• Opa Reimer was not heard from again. It is assumed he was killed by the Nazi soldiers.

• Frau Gosau (the woman who gave the Reimers a bed and some dishes when they relocated in Dollerup) moved back to her hometown after the war. She did visit Ruth and Kenneth in the states.

• Neighbors told the family that the Polish people and the Allies found the buried trunk with furs and rifles right away. The Rosentaler china was also missing from where it had been buried near the lilac bush.

• The Reimer family was never reimbursed for the farms they owned in West Prussia, even though the government had told its citizens that reimbursements would be given.

• After the war, Oma Hintz married Volchert, who was a widower. The Reimer family owned a double house in Espelkamp which had living arrangements upstairs and downstairs. Oma and her husband lived in one part and the Reimers lived in the other.

• The Danish nurse who saved the life of Heidi was never able to be thanked. When Mamma shared the story with Heidi, it was so many years later that it would have been impossible to locate the nurse. Mamma told Heidi about the nurse not long before she died in 1995. No one knows why she never told her children. No one knows for certain if Pappa knew.

• After Ruth came to America, she was privileged to meet the Daniel Bontrager family from Indiana and thank them personally for the many items they sent to her family after the war. Without those care packages, her Mamma said, they would not have survived.

Appendix A—The War and Its Effects

Ruth has given her story numerous times over the years—many of them not recorded. At an event in March 1977, Kenneth summarized Ruth's pilgrimage in a talk he gave. He also shared on this same theme in 2010. The notes from these two events are shared here.

1. War is not the way to solve problems. Instead of war solving problems, it only creates new problems: widows, fatherless, and maimed (both psychological and physical—the trauma of seeing bloodshed and the awful violence caused by warfare.)

2. The innocent suffer in war regardless of age and sex. Not only because of the suffering in World War II, and this is where Ruth was a victim of war, but such suffering is going on continuously throughout our world. I guess if there is one thing that overwhelms me over the years, it is how people have been pushed around and their personal lives have been restricted because of war.

3. God can and will lead amidst all the turmoil. World War II created heartache and havoc for not only German people, but for the world. Adolf Hitler used propaganda to the hilt. Ruth learned that there is only one safe place to be, and that is to give one's heart to the Lord Jesus Christ, accept His Word for what it is, and develop a simple trusting faith. If we get that right, we are in for a good life and a good future. It may not all be wonderful, but it will be good.

Appendix B—Glossary

Alvin J. Miller. 1883-1981. Alvin J. Miller, great-uncle of Kenneth Yoder, served on the Friend's Service Committee for reconstruction and relief work after World War I. Miller was commissioned a captain in the American Red Cross, but transferred to the staff of MCC when Mennonites became organized to help the starving in Russia. Miller negotiated the contract with the Russian government for MCC and became the director of MCC's extensive Russian relief in 1921-1926. Miller had working relations with Herbert Hoover's American Relief Organization.[67]

Conscientious Objectors: A conscientious objector is a person who requests to be relieved of participating in military service because of personal convictions. He refuses to participate in military operations because of his acceptance of Christ's commandment to love our enemies, do good to those who hate us, and pray for those who abuse us [Luke 6:27-36.] The U.S. government provided an alternative service opportunity through I-W service. In June 1951, the U.S. Congress passed the Universal Military Training and Service Act which established the I-W program. One of the ways in which I-W differed from Civilian Public Service during World War II was that it allowed conscientious objectors to perform alternative service overseas. General Lewis B. Hershey visited the PAX site in Germany and approved the program for alternative service credit. The members of the program financed their services with a $75 fee, either paid by them or their home congregation.[68]

PAX – the Greek word for Peace [peace, quietness, rest, one] developed into a program operated between 1951 and 1976. The idea for PAX came from Calvin Redekop and Paul Peachey who worked for Mennonite Central Committee at the time, as a way for Mennonites to help rebuild postwar Europe and serve as a voluntary service option in the draft. Political developments focused the project on providing resettlement housing for

---

[67] Ivan J. and Della Miller, "The Life and Passing of Alvin J. Miller," *The Casselman Chronicle* (1981), Numbers 3 and 4, pp. 2-3.

[68] "The Pax Program." Wikipedia, Wikimedia Foundation, 24 June 2018, en.wikipedia.org/wiki/The_Pax_Program.

the Danzig Mennonite refugees. The first team arrived in Espelkamp, Germany, on April 6, 1951, and lived in renovated gas munitions bunkers. Pax provided housing for 270 German families, as well as a Mennonite Meetinghouse for the community. The PAX Program stopped sending volunteers in 1973, and the program was closed by 1976. Reasons for closing the program included the fact that the original purpose of refugee assistance had ended by 1960, and the draft was terminated by the end of 1972. By the time the program stopped sending volunteers in 1973, PAX had sent about 1,180 men to 42 different countries around the world. The efforts of those who might have served in PAX were directed towards other MCC programs.[69]

I-W Service. In the U.S., virtually all males ages 18-25 were required to register with the Selective Service. From 1947-1973, registered men were drafted to fill vacancies in the armed forces that could not be filled through voluntary means. There were different classifications of service. The I-W draft code referred to a conscientious objector who performed civilian work contributing to the maintenance of national health, safety, or interest or to one who completed such work. The "I" in I-W is pronounced "one" and not "eye".

Mennonite Central Committee (MCC) is a worldwide ministry of Anabaptist churches. Its goal is to share God's love and compassion for all in the name of Christ by responding to basic human needs and working for peace and justice. The U.S. Headquarters is in Akron, Pennsylvania. In Canada, the headquarters is in Winnipeg, Manitoba. The web site is www.mcc.org. MCC has five areas of focus:

1. Caring for the lives and futures of uprooted and other vulnerable people.
2. Providing water, food and shelter first in times of hunger, disaster and conflict; then education and ways to earn income.
3. Working with churches and communities to prevent violence and promote peace and justice.
4. Investing in opportunities for young people to serve in Canada, the U.S., and around the world.
5. Serving with humility and in partnership to meet local needs with local solutions.

---

[69] *Ibid.*

MCC was founded on September 27, 1920. by Mennonites in North America. Its purpose was to provide relief to those in countries where famines and wars had devastated the land. MCC was established as a vehicle through which they could bring aid to fellow believers following the devastations of famine and revolution in Russia. From there, MCC moved into other countries, including war-torn Europe at the end of World War II.

Across the U.S., sewing circles from Anabaptist churches compiled care packages and Christmas bundles sent to refugees. The Christmas bundles were "wrapped" with a bath towel and closed with safety pins. Inside the bundles were items such as soap, wash cloths, toothbrushes, and toothpaste. By closing the "bundles" with safety pins, even the pins could be used by the refugees. Care packages were compiled by families and churches with more specific items, especially if the families knew the needs of those receiving the packages (as was the case with the Reimer family and the Daniel Bontrager family, Goshen, Indiana).

The Daniel Bontrager family from Goshen, Indiana, about 1955. Two more children were born to the family after 1955.

Bibliography

Berenbaum, Michael. "Kristallnacht." *Encyclopedia Britannica,* Encyclopædia Britannica, Inc., 20 Dec. 2018, www.britannica.com/event/Kristallnacht.

Bontrager, Linford. Photo of Bontrager family, circa 1955-1956.

Brunk, Emily. *Espelkamp.* The Mennonite Central Committee, 1951.

Cowper, William, Timeless Truths Free Online Library | books, sheet music, midi, and more. "God Moves in a Mysterious Way." library.timelesstruths. org/music/God_Moves_in_a_Mysterious_Way/.

De Bewoonde Vrouw, www.doorbraak.eu/gebladerte/30142v01.htm.

Deutsch-Englisch-Wörterbuch, www.dict.cc/german-english/Soldbuch.html.

"Die Lorelei." *Puer Natus in Bethlehem / A Child Is Born in Bethlehem Gospel Christian Songs Free mp3 Midi Download,* ingeb.org/Lieder/ichweiss.html.

Editors, History.com. "Yalta Conference." *History.com,* A&E Television Networks, 29 Oct. 2009, www.history.com/topics/world-war-ii/yalta-conference.

"Gedser." *Estonia—Wikitravel,* wikitravel.org/en/Gedser. November 26, 2018. https://en.wikipedia.org/wiki/Gedser

Gingerich, John (1911-2010). "The Ruth Reimer Yoder Story", Unpublished, 1977. Interviews in German with Johannes and Gerda Reimer are transcribed into this story. Gingerich was hired by Kenneth Yoder to visit the Reimers in Germany, conduct the interview and write the story from the interview.

"Hasselø Plantage." *Wikipedia,* Wikimedia Foundation, 20 Mar. 2017, en.wikipedia.org/wiki/Hassel%C3%B8_Plantage.

"Hectare." *Wikipedia*, Wikimedia Foundation, 26 Dec. 2018, en.wikipedia.org/wiki/Hectare.

"Ich Bin Klein - Germany." *Mama Lisa's World of Children and International Culture*, www.mamalisa.com/?t=es&p=2865.

"Laboe Naval Memorial." *Wikipedia*, Wikimedia Foundation, 14 Dec. 2018, en.wikipedia.org/wiki/Laboe_Naval_Memorial.

"Mennonite Nazis:" *Charles Spurgeon's Home Life / Home History / The Heartbeat of the Remnant*, www.ephrataministries.org/remnant-2012-11-mennonite-nazis.a5w.

"Nazi Songs." *Wikipedia*, Wikimedia Foundation, 13 Sept. 2018, simple.wikipedia.org/wiki/Nazi_songs.

"Oksbøl Refugee Camp." *Wikipedia*, Wikimedia Foundation, 26 Nov. 2018, en.wikipedia.org/wiki/Oksb%C3%B8l_Refugee_Camp.

Reimer, Johannes and Gerda. "Collection of Letters Translated from German to English." Letters written in German from Johannes and Gerda Reimer (Dollerup and Espelkamp, Germany) to the Daniel S. Bontrager family (Goshen, Ind., USA) and translated into English by John E. Gingerich, Hartville, Ohio. The 26 letters are dated from February 2, 1947 to December 9, 1956.

"Rügen." *Wikipedia*, Wikimedia Foundation, 19 Nov. 2018, en.wikipedia.org/wiki/R%C3%BCgen.

Schrock, Reagan. *Mennonite Nazis and the Two-Kingdom Concept*. Thesis written for graduation at SMBI, Harrisville, Pa., in 2014.

"Schutzstaffel." *Wikipedia*, Wikimedia Foundation, 10 Jan. 2019, en.wikipedia.org/wiki/Schutzstaffel.

"Stutthof Concentration Camp." *Wikipedia*, Wikimedia Foundation, 2 Jan. 2019, en.wikipedia.org/wiki/Stutthof_concentration_camp.

"The Pax Program." *Wikipedia*, Wikimedia Foundation, 24 June 2018, en.wikipedia.org/wiki/The_Pax_Program.

The Thompson Exhaustive Topical Bible: King James Version. B.B. Kirkbridde Bible Co., 1997.

Tischer, Rolf. "Vom Himmel in Die Tiefsten Klüfte - Klassisch - Gedichte." *Weihnachtsstadt*, www.weihnachtsstadt.de/gedichte/klassisch/vom-himmel-in-die-klufte.htm.

Viking Burial Customs, Danishnet, 19 Dec. 2018, www.danishnet.com/travel-denmark/kolding.

Yoder, Ruth R. "A Personal Testimony as a Tribute to the 75th Anniversary of Mennonite Central Committee." *The Newsletter of The Casselman Valley Conservative Mennonite Churches*, vol. 43, no. 14, 9 July.

Yoder, Ruth R. "My Life." Grantsville MD, 0AD. This hand-written nine-page summary was written in preparation for sharing her story at an event and is unpublished.

Yoder, Ruth R. "My Story." Grantsville MD, 0AD. This hand-written seven-page summary was written for the Yoder family and is unpublished.

Yoder, Ruth R. "The Story of Ruth Yoder - Her Life Experience in Nazi Germany." Bradley Maust, Mar. 2018. Track 1: 1962 at Maple Glen Mennonite Church, Grantsville, MD Track 2: "We Were a Refugee Family". 1963 at Conservative Mennonite Conference Goshen, IN. Track 3: circa 2010 at SMBI, Harrisonville, Pa.

Ruth Yoder today holding the wooden box as described and pictured on page 140.